IF IT WEREN'T FOR THE HONOR — I'D RATHER HAVE WALKED

Previously untold tales of the journey to the ADA

by **Jan Little**

BROOKLINE BOOKS

ISBN 1-57129-026-5

Library of Congress Cataloging-In-Publication Data
Little, Jan, 1939-
    If it weren't for the honor--I'd rather have walked : previously untold tales of the journey to the ADA / by Jan Little.
        p.   cm.
    ISBN 1-57129-026-5 (pbk.)
    1. Little, Jan, 1939-   . 2. Physically handicapped--United States--Biography.   3. Sociology of disability--United States.
4. Discrimination against the handicapped--United States.
5. Handicapped--Civil Rights--United States.   I. Title.
HV3013.L58A3   1996
362.4 ' 1 ' 092--dc20
[B]

                                    96-17461
                                         CIP

Printed in Canada by Best Book Manufacturing, Louiseville, Québec.

Published by
BROOKLINE BOOKS
P.O. Box 1047 • Cambridge, Massachusetts 02238

Foreword

Living in Illinois for over half of my life led me to be a great admirer of Abraham Lincoln. One of my favorite Lincoln tales is a story about a man who incurred the wrath of the citizens of a town. These folks treated him to a coating of tar, covered by feathers, then escorted him out of town on a rail. According to Lincoln, when asked how he felt about such treatment, the man replied, "If it hadn't been for the honor, I'd have rather walked."

Living in a wheelchair for nearly 40 years has left me with the same feeling many times.

A lot of progress has been made over those 40 years. This progress has been made because of the trials and tribulations, efforts, joys and agonies of hundreds of people. Some of these people had disabilities. Some did not.

Some of them have enjoyed a great deal of publicity and credit for changing the lives of people with disabilities. Others are pretty much unknown.

This book is mostly about the ones who haven't had their stories told. They, rather than the people you've seen on the TV and in the news, made the real changes. Their stories are told through the eyes of a person who was lucky enough to be there when good things happened.

WARNING: This book contains opinions of the author that aren't very popular with federal agencies, do-gooders who've dedicated their lives to helping poor cripples and anyone who claims having a disability is either an endless struggle, a courageous act or an inspiration to all.

contents

prologue

Who elected me to tell this story?

If you read the popular press, watch television or come across any of the increasing number of publications, exhibitions or computer networks aimed at the segment of the population that has a disability, you're likely to come to one of several conclusions. You may think that the signing of the Americans with Disability Act (ADA) suddenly brought millions of people with disabilities out of whatever closet or institution they had been occupying. Or, you might think that it's only in the past few years that people with disabilities have begun to live a life that's pretty much "normal" — except that they use a wheelchair or talk with an electronic voice or walk down the street preceded by a white cane. You might even think, "well, that's pretty brave and courageous of that person — even though she uses a wheelchair, she managed to visit Yellowstone Park last summer."

Well, the ADA did increase the acknowledged number of people with disabilities (PWDs). In order to put together what the advertising and sales people call a "significant mass," the people who wanted to sell the ADA to congress pointed out that there are a lot of people with "hidden disabilities." For example, Ron Santo, the former Chicago Cub star, has a hidden disability. He's been shooting up daily with insulin since he was a kid. A goodly portion of today's rock music stars have a hidden disability. They've stopped shooting up with heroin or other mind-benders and qualify as recovering substance abusers under the ADA. Before the campaign to enact the ADA, very few people had enough interest to inquire how many people with disabilities there were in the United States. What's worse, even fewer people could tell anyone who asked how many there were. Even the ADA figure of "over 43 million" was an educated guess.

And it is true that PWDs have become more visible on the streets and in the mass media in the past few years. For one thing, there are more PWDs who can get out and do things because trauma treatment and modern medicine are saving people who would have died a couple of decades ago. The law of averages means more PWDs will be out in public because there are more people with disabilities. An overall decrease in architectural barriers and an overall enlightenment in public attitude has also increased the number of people with disabilities now seen in public. It was hard for a person with a disability to be visible when they couldn't cross the street from their house because there were no curb cuts. It's also become socially unacceptable and politically incorrect to stone people with disabilities or use them in circus freak shows.

As to the brave and courageous bit, that's something that PWDs will be stuck with until everyone who thinks getting up and leaving the house in the morning is brave and courageous meets a real, live individual PWD and finds out how cowardly, surly, lazy and thoroughly unlikable we can be — just like everyone else. I wish I could remember the name of the woman addressing a meeting of people "dedicated to helping the disabled" who, unlike the members of the audience, knew what a disability was because she had one. When asked what the most courageous thing she did, she replied, "Decide to wear a pair of panty hose — then struggle into them." Maybe I liked that remark because I know first-hand what it's like to lie on your back on the bed, get one leg of the panty hose scrunched down so it will fit over your toes, catch your leg with one hand and get the toes and the panty hose in the same area. Invariably, the first leg goes on OK, but, just as your getting the second leg nicely started up your limb, you punch a hole in the panty hose and start over. The moral to that story — if there is one — is that what looks like courage is really pretty boring, everyday stuff.

What looks like new opportunities and achievements for PWDs is usually something that's been done before in the past 40 years — but didn't make the six o'clock news. Stories about "the first person in a wheelchair to go to regular college classes," if printed after 1948, are the result of a writer who didn't do the proper research. Stories about companies started by a person with a disability that hires PWDs and makes a competitive product, if printed after 1948, have ignored quite a number of similar companies in the past including PAMCO in Bensenville, IL, and Abilities, Inc. on Long Island.

Some of us who've been disabled long enough to have progressed from "cripple" to "handicapped" to "physically challenged" and back to cripple know that there have always been a lot of people with disabilities who have gone about their business and done what they wanted to do even though they did have a disability. They just didn't make the Sunday supplement of the local newspaper or the six o'clock news. They didn't campaign for any titles, like "Handicapped Man of the Year." They just did their thing.

It's been my privilege to know many of these people. Indeed, I've been a partner-in-crime with some of the best of the wild men and women who broke down the barriers so that the person who enters PWD status today has it easier.

Of course, I elected myself to tell the stories of those barrier break-downs and limit to what-a-PWD-can-do stretching. I had encouragement from some of the others. "OK," I said. "But this book isn't going to be about what Jan Little did — only what she observed or was part of and there won't be any bravery or courage or groaning" — except, possibly by the reader.

"You have to tell people who you are and what you were doing that put you in all the places and events you describe," said the friendly publisher, Mr. Cheever.

"Aw, Ray," the author replied. "Unlike most people who've just gotten their first AARP notice in the mail, I don't even know what I want to be when I grow up. As for what I've done — I've worked — mostly in journalism, marketing and that sort of thing."

"More specific," comes the terse reply of the publisher.

So, here's what I've done.

Grew up on a farm in Wisconsin. Went to the University of Illinois in Champaign-Urbana where I fell in love with wheelchair sports, running student organizations and causing trouble and, incidentally, earned bachelors and masters degrees in journalism and communications. Concentrated on sports more than making a living for about five years, so I wandered around the world with the USA wheelchair team. Went on to become an editor of trade magazines in Chicago, then became the head of a small national company that developed and distributed products to let people with disabilities get on with their lives. While I was with that company, I played at helping with work that led to legislation in Washington and got included in the founding of an international rehabilitation engineering society. Then I was hired by a large manufacturer of wheelchairs in their marketing department and traveled around the U.S. and Canada for them until they "down-sized." Being an equal opportunity company, they down-sized me right along with a bunch of other execs. Like many of my contemporaries — who find themselves out of a job frequently as companies try to decide what they're going to be when they grow up — I've done consulting, writing and anything else legal to pay the mortgages — since I seem to have made buying condominiums a hobby.

Then, I got myself hired to design a national center to co-ordinate how PWDs get the state-of-the-art technology that lets them — to quote the writers of the ADA — level the playing field. After five years, the Board of Directors of the project said that they couldn't understand why people with disabilities didn't just get the government to buy what they need and, what's more, the BOD couldn't understand the whole area of assistive technology and was having a lot of trouble getting philanthropic organizations to give them money to initiate the project. They decided to do things they could understand — like send little crippled kids to camp and teach people to put switches on toys. So I'm back to holding the hands of inventors of great new products that can make life easier for PWDs, writing articles that tell the rehab equipment industry what a mess the federal programs have made of the industry and generally being a trouble maker — a role that, like a locust — re-cycles about every seven years in my life.

Now, wasn't that pretty boring? The rest of the book — being about people other than me — I hope is much more fun.

Note:
Special thanks to Tim Nugent and Chuck Chevillon who patiently read the manuscript to make sure my notes and memories matched the real events.

Dedication

Along the journey traveled by people with disabilities
— which began with PWDs being locked in institutions or put on the street to beg
and progressed to PWDs being the focus of the nation's most
all-inclusive equal rights legislation, the ADA—
there have been thousands of people who quietly went about living their lives
and making their contributions despite the fact
that they were considered disabled.
The progress — and this book — would not have happened without those people.
This book is dedicated to all the people who have made accessible roads across the
hostile
frontiers of prejudice and misunderstanding;
to all the people who would not accept the word "can't" and
to all the people who took me by the hand, opened the doors and
let me share their triumphs and their stories.

chapter I

Getting into the disability scene

Since the rest of this book relates to people I met and events that happened because I use a wheelchair, it seems necessary to explain why I use a chair. Besides, if you're writing a book about having a disability, it's absolutely mandatory to put in the part about the onset. Of course, acquiring a disability is a traumatic, life-changing occurrence for anyone, but I've never quite understood why writers feel it is necessary to take the reader through each minute of "how I coped with becoming a crip" in agonizing detail. The most interesting thing that happened while I was involved in becoming paralyzed was that Dwight D. Eisenhower got elected President.

Anyway, here's the dramatic, obligatory story of how one person was initiated into having a disability. In 1952, polio took it's last gigantic sweep across the United States before Dr. Salk and Dr. Sabine discovered vaccines that would end the epidemics that terrorized families each summer. In Wisconsin, we thought we were through the worst when, in October, our rural township was hit hard by the virus. My cousin was sent to Madison, not expected to survive the bulbar polio which paralyzed his lungs. The Chicago Board of Health was closing dairy farm after dairy farm as members of the farm family were diagnosed with polio.

On the 13th of October, I got polio.

Our family doctor had gone on vacation and the brand new, young doctor finally agreed that I should be taken to the hospital since I could no longer stand up or swallow water — and my fever of 105 could have heated the house.

Mercy Hospital, in Janesville, was a general hospital and, typical of small hospitals in rural areas, did not specialize in any particular areas of medicine. As it turned out, that was probably to my advantage. The sisters and nurses used a lot of common sense mixed in with treatments they learned about from polio centers — like the Sister Kenny Institute in Minneapolis which wrapped people who had polio in pieces of wool just removed from boiling water. The nurses explained that this was supposed to ease the muscle pain. Even at age 13, I could figure out that what it did was take your mind off the pain of polio by substituting a more intense pain. I've had a life-long sympathy with lobsters after that experience. OK — that takes care of the agonizing part.

In Janesville, if you had a really good case of polio, you got sent to Madison or Milwaukee. If you were really interesting — or a total mess — you got sent to Warm Springs, Georgia. I was lucky. I didn't get sent anywhere. For one thing, the facilities were so full that year that there were no beds available. Realistically, the Sisters of Mercy and their nurses, who worked around the clock caring for us, probably did as much as the facilities that specialized in polio. Fur-

2

thermore, my family preferred to deal with this crisis face to face. We'd always solved our problems ourselves and, by gum, we could solve this one. That takes care of the "my days in the rehab center" part.

So I went home to the farm. One of my aunts — who none of the family really liked very much anyway — told anyone who would listen that my family was too cheap to send me away for treatment. There could be some truth in that. Dad's ancestors came from Scotland and family legend has it that some of them worked their way over and then forgot to catch the ship back to the British Isles. Actually, the fact that frugality is the strongest genetic trait in my family has stood me in good stead. If you come off having a disability, it helps you through the tight spots to be able to live on less money than anyone other than the people who sleep on grates in big cities.

Oh yeah, I came out of the hospital totally paralyzed from the chest down, and my right shoulder and upper arm and left hand were pretty weak. The orthopedic surgeon who had taken over my case told Dad we could try braces and crutches, but not to expect a whole lot. That turned out to be good advice. Other families spent tons of money to send their kids to rehab centers where, after many months, they were convinced that they shouldn't expect a whole lot.

While others who had had polio were sweating away in physical therapy departments, my family developed our own rehab program. Everyone worked on the farm. Before I had polio, my sister, Judy, and I were as good at being hired hands as any. Farms are marvelous places for kids to grow up. Farm work comes in various levels of difficulty so a kid can start as soon she can pick up eggs and work up to bigger jobs. It's not too long before you're big enough to hold a pitch fork and fluff up the straw in the cows' stalls while they're on their break outside.

Dad, still remembering the 40 rods of fence I took out with the Farmall, always reminds me that I wasn't too good at driving a tractor. But, I could feed pigs, chickens and sheep. I could catch grain from the combines as the men harvested and unload it into the elevators that took it up to the bins. I was also pretty good at trudging through the snow on cold winter nights to bottle feed lambs whose mothers didn't want them. When I ended up paralyzed, Mom replaced me at my chores in addition to the time she already spent in the barns and fields.

This opened up an opportunity for what we in the rehabilitation technology field thirty years later heralded as Job Site Modification and Job Accommodation. Mom figured out that the kitchen was pretty accessible. I could reach the sink to do dishes and reach the stove to cook. Farms, like restaurants, feed people three times a day. No bowl of cold cereal or sandwich for the people who've moved 800 pounds of manure in the last two hours! Mom had also been raised to believe that not only is cleanliness next to godliness, everything that gets washed must be ironed. If you were in an accident would you want the doctor to see that your bra and panties hadn't been ironed? Obviously, whoever invented ironing boards made them so they could be at a good level for a kid sitting in a wheelchair.

The real stroke of genius though was gardening. As poor farm folk — an image my family carefully clung to even though my grandfather held mortgages on many of the farms in Rock County and owned more than a couple of farms in his time — we grew our food. We canned, froze, pickled, cold-packed or made into relish, preserves, jams and jellies everything except the 30-plus cats that shared the farm with us. We had two freezers, 90 feet of shelves for canned goods and a root cellar as big as a Chicago studio apartment. Had nuclear attack been a threat in those days, we could have held out for a decade.

With us, gardening was what you did to relax after a full day of farming. The spring after I had polio, Dad carefully laid the garden out with the rows far enough apart to let a wheelchair through without mashing the peas and beans. Then, Mom cut the handle of a hoe to a good length for someone sitting down and, by backing between rows, I could get rid of those weeds. The fact that I could only get out of one end of the garden in my chair guaranteed at least two rows got hoed on each outing.

Picking strawberries was a much better work-out than anything you could do on a mat in the physical therapy department. Strawberry plants are short. To get the berries, it is necessary to get down on the ground. The results were a) learning to get out of chair onto the ground, b) crawling — or in my case, dragging my butt — on grass and c) wonderful strawberry shortcakes, pies and jams.

Thirty years before therapeutic horticulture came into vogue, my relatives, neighbors and probably a few people we didn't even know we knew, took it upon themselves to make a horticulturist of me. I ended up with 20 rose bushes in my rose garden because I was inundated with the bushes or cash to buy them. One of our neighbors owned an iris farm. I was probably the only kid in Rock County with 1,000 iris plants. Not only was this something we could do as a family, we got so involved that a local bank named our farm as one of the best landscaping efforts in the county. And no one else even had a chance to win the prizes for flowers at the county fair.

Not only was this form of rehabilitation fun, it seemed to work. Dr. Bob Jackson who, as medical director of Craig Rehabilitation Hospital in Denver, Colorado, broke all the rules to get people back to real lives after disability, became one of my good friends. He tore up a rehab medicine meeting once by using me as an example of rehab in context with a person's lifestyle.

"My friend here," he told the audience, "fails to fit the role and image we assign to post-polio quadriplegics. The silly woman doesn't know what she's supposed to do or not do. It was her great good fortune to become disabled before we perfected rehabilitation treatment. When she found out what her limits were, she'd already passed them."

My "rehabilitation" was what results when people don't know the rules. My family, friend and neighbors didn't have much of an idea about what people who are paralyzed could or couldn't do. They pretty much believed that helplessness and dependency didn't put food on the table, though. Fortunately, there were no books about how to be disabled. They wouldn't have read them anyway. They didn't even read the stuff the county agent brought them about hog cholera.

There was the matter of schooling. Everyone knew that book learning was important and kids needed to learn. Shortly after I came home from the hospital, one of our neighbors, Ann Sullivan, appeared at the back door. Before marrying and having seven kids, Ann had taught in some of the many all-eight-grades-in-one-room schools where most

Wisconsin citizens got their education. Not only had Ann been responsible for teaching every subject plus music and art for all eight grades, she had to get to school early enough each morning to get the stove fired up so the building would be warm when the students arrived.

Ann had been an influence on my sister's and my life since we entered first grade. Like many of the Irish wives in our community, Ann was clever at stretching her husband's meager paycheck to cover the needs of her family. She knew that, even though the kids on the farms in the area didn't have much money spent on them, they could have the chance to do anything they wanted if they had the basics — clean clothes and an education. As though her seven children — all of whom grew up to be outstanding citizens — weren't enough, Ann took on the task of preparing all of the kids in the Mouat one-room school for the day when they would have to "go to town" for high school.

I'm not sure we even really knew what a movie was when Ann piled us in her car and took us to see "Snow White." We behaved, too. In our area, kids didn't have their own parties, they tagged along to card parties and dances with their parents. Ann sent us scurrying to the attic for Halloween costumes, taught us how to trick-or-treat without tipping over outhouses and was responsible for some of our first lessons in being civilized.

It wasn't surprising that Ann took my situation as a personal challenge. As she put it, "For Heaven Sake, it's her legs that don't work, not her mind."

Ann gathered up the books and lesson plans from Mouat School, took her toddler, Jane, by the hand and set up school in our living room. In those days, we respected teachers. Actually, we were afraid of them because if we went astray, not only would the teacher lecture you, but by the time you got home, she'd have let your parents know you'd been bad and you had to face them. I doubt there was any child abuse in our farm community, but us kids weren't about to find out what happened if you sassed a grown-up.

I never was good in arithmetic. I didn't even like the subject. It was easier to be good in arithmetic than face Ann glaring over her glasses at me. If I did well, I could read any book I wanted to — and, somehow, the Valentine and St. Patrick Day parties for Mouat School got moved to our living room.

For decades, the Rock County 4-H Fair was the largest in the world. It even made the National Geographic one year. Our lives revolved around it. It taught boys to raise animals and crops. It taught girls to cook, sew, decorate their homes and care for families. We were pretty far into sexual equality. Girls could raise and show animals — except for bulls, which were considered too hard to handle. Boys could take cooking or sewing, but they were considered somewhat more than a little odd.

The 4-H Fair was where you could win enough prize money and sell enough livestock to buy a pretty snazzy wardrobe for high school with a little left over. It was the place where boys and girls sneaked off to the hay racks above the animal pens to experiment with a little kissing. Those experiments must have been pretty successful. When you go through the barns at the Fair today, you see the same family names above the pens that were there when I was a kid. Of course, it's the grandchildren now.

As with school, my family and neighbors never considered that I wouldn't continue in 4-H. Polio was certainly not enough reason to quit before your 20th birthday. Twenty years later, 4-H, like the Boy and Girl Scouts, would set up clubs for kids with disabilities. We didn't have those kind of resources in Rock County. Besides, what did polio have to do with how well I could bake cookies, sew or raise flowers. It certainly was no reason for me not to assume my responsibilities as a Junior Leader when I reached 16.

Having had polio didn't inspire Aunt Fay to cut much slack either. "Good Godfrey, girl," she would say as she inspected my latest attempt at a bound button hole,

"It's not supposed to look like a pig's eye. Do it over — and don't try it on that expensive wool until you've got it — cotton's cheaper."

Sewing machines were controlled by a lever you pushed with your knee. No problem. We figured out that I could push my leg against the lever with one hand while I guided the fabric with the other. You just had to pay a little more attention.

Judy quickly figured out that, since I wasn't going to be much good at showing my sheep, I should help her with the ponies.

"Here," she explained as she positioned her favorite mare in front of my chair. "You braid Dolly's mane and tail so they'll be nice and curly for the show. Dolly, stand still and be careful because Sis is in a wheelchair now — and she can't move too quick."

Maybe the ponies understood what Judy told them. They let me lead them, even though they would pull away from other people, and behaved gently around me — except for the foals, who would sneak in and chew the rubber tips of the wheelchair brake handles.

Dolly won the Grand Championship that summer. Mom eventually forgave Judy and I for "borrowing" a home permanent and her best shampoo to improve Dolly's chances for winning. Dad pointed out that he didn't think it was a good idea to have me ride on a float built on a hay wagon, pulled by a tractor driven by a kid just learning to drive. But, since I'd won prizes in art at school, it was OK for me to become chief float designer, backdrop painter and creator of barn displays.

By the Fall after I'd had polio, I was just another 4-H kid — swinging between being a good kid and a pain in the ass. It was pretty incidental that I ran around the fairgrounds and got in trouble using a wheelchair instead of my legs.

In spite of the fact that I was accepted back into our community, there was still the pressure to learn to walk. Walking was proof that you had worked hard and overcome your disability. Wheelchairs were associated with old or sick people. Not that we've overcome that view in our society. People still come up to me and say, "Wouldn't you rather walk than use a wheelchair?" or "I had an aunt in a wheelchair once, but, fortunately, she died."

Outside of our farm community being in a wheelchair carried a fair amount of shame. Soon after I came home from the hospital, the local Farm Bureau group sponsored a concert by a group from the WLS Barn Dance. Our neighbors helped get me into the hall and I got autographed pictures of the group. But there were people who criticized my parents for "taking a child like that out in public."

chapter 2

If you try
(or have faith, or eat a
special diet, etc. ,etc.)
you will WALK

Through the years, as I've talked to other people who had polio, I find we share one thing in common. Down deep, we wonder if we've tried hard enough. After all, we never learned to walk.

Even in rural Wisconsin, there was pressure to work hard and learn to walk. Janesville had no physical therapy departments, so Mom would drive me to a town 20 miles away several times a week to be treated by Miss Wolfgram, a physical therapist who loved treating children. Julane Wolfgram would prop me up on braces that reached to my waist, re-enforced by a corset that reached to my armpits and we would practice walking. Usually I imitated a tree. I'd sway back and forth a few frantic moments, then crash to the ground, maintaining a straight position until I hit the ground.

Miss Wolfgram also dunked me in hydrotherapy and used electrical stimulation. Back in those days, no one knew you could modulate the current used in muscle stimulation. The early units delivered a jolt just below the strength of the electric chair.

Nothing worked — except me and Miss Wolfgram.

Life certainly wasn't perfect, but our family managed to ignore most of the uninvited advice from people who thought we "certainly should do something about that child not walking." We didn't listen to the lady who swore that if I ate enough alfalfa, I'd recover or the neighbor lady who kept wandering through musing about how I could be so punished for my sins when I hadn't even had enough time to commit that many sins. We really didn't pay any attention to one of my aunts — the one none of us really liked — when she periodically insisted that if my Dad would just set the house on fire, I'd learn to walk so I could get out.

Overall, we had the support of our family and neighbors. It came as a bitter experience to be confronted by the absolute refusal of the superintendent of the city school system to let me continue my education at the high school level.

Dad claims that the steam calliope was invented by someone who listened to one of Mom's female ancestors expressing distress. Mom gave credibility to Dad's theory when she returned from a meeting with the city superintendent of schools. Between sobs, she managed to relay the superintendent's message that, since the high school was a multi-story building, the classes would have to be re-arranged and that was not convenient. He evidently went on to express his belief that since her kid was always going to be crippled, it didn't make any sense to waste time educating me. Besides, think of how depressing it would be for the other kids to have to look at me every day. And, No! The city couldn't accept home tutoring.

The superintendent underestimated Mom. Like a she-bear protecting her cub, she charged. She couldn't go above his head, so she went below him and she played dirty doing it. She parked herself outside the office of Ken Bick. Ken was principal of the high school and had taught Dad in class. Ken also kept track of every student who ever attended his school — sending cards to former students every time he learned of a significant event in their life until he was over 90. Ken restored order to the school by promising Mom a solution to the problem, helping her out of the building and tucking her into her car.

The solution Ken found wasn't too comforting to Dad. "He's sending out Pop Strong and his wife to tutor Jan!", Dad wailed. "Do you realize that Pop Strong is the only teacher who ever threw me out of class?"

Lauren "Pop" Strong and his wife, Frieda, soon became a part of our family. Not only did they declare themselves adoptive grandparents, they taught me math, science, English, history and the other subjects being studied by students at my grade level. The only time there was a problem was the day Mr. Strong supplemented the biology lesson by tucking a grass snake into his pocket for me to play with as part of the reptile study. Mom broke the four-minute mile record long before it was done officially — and refused to let Pop Strong in the house from that day on without turning his pockets inside out.

The battle wasn't won. The state of Wisconsin, responding to pressure from the city schools, sent a psychologist out

13

from Madison to prove that I was retarded. The poor man never caught on to the fact that my scores rose with each test he administered. He used the same test each time and never considered that a devious kid like me could read upside down as he scored the tests.

By the time I reached my junior year, the city had built a new high school with most of the classrooms on one level. This removed the excuse that I couldn't get to class. Besides, by that time, the school board was weary of listening to the uproar about keeping me out of school that was coming from everyone from my family to the local priest. I was finally admitted.

We'd promised that I would ask for no special privileges. Going to the bathroom turned out to be a special privilege. No doorways in the girls restrooms were wide enough for me to get through in my wheelchair. It is possible to not use the bathroom for six or seven hours — if you don't drink any fluids.

In spite of the incident when my homeroom teacher apologized to the rest of the class for having to be in the room with me, good things happened. Not only did Lowell Wilson, the physics teacher, welcome me into his laboratory, he encouraged me to work in the visual aids department, the hang-out for the science crowd.

Kids in high school in those days were only beginning to learn prejudice and discrimination. Actually, we didn't have a lot of people to discriminate against in our little town. You were either Catholic or Protestant. We had two Jewish families, but they belonged to the Congregational church.

Like the rest of the kids at Janesville Senior High, some of the other kids liked me and some didn't. We formed our cliques and carried on like teenagers. I ended up in forensics and debate. Roger and Bill, my debate team partners, managed to carry me up and down stairways in schools all over southeastern Wisconsin and only drop me a little way one time.

The end of any high school student's senior year is a trauma. We were going our separate ways. While the kids I'd hung out with in school talked excitedly about being accepted to the University of Wisconsin, the Ivy League and the Seven Sisters, Notre Dame and St. Olaf's, I became more quiet. The school counselor gently broke the news to me that no college or university would accept a person in a wheelchair as a full-time, residential student.

chapter 3

We're loyal to you, Illinois

It didn't make sense to anyone involved — including some of the teachers at Janesville Senior High — to give up on college. I'd won some scholarship money and my Great Aunt Ann, both the family matriarch and rebel, had given me money to go to college. If nothing else, no one who knew her would have considered not doing what Aunt Annie said.

Once again, the state of Wisconsin got into the act. Of course, people in wheelchairs didn't go to universities, they assured me. The fact that I wanted to go and had no intention of considering a full-time attendant caused them to mumble about the need for intensive psychiatric counseling. Again, a state psychologist trudged out to the boondocks from Madison and tried to explain life to me.

The purpose of the Wisconsin Division of Vocational Rehabilitation, he pointed out, was to provide means of training for people with disabilities who had a chance of becoming employed. What did I think I could do for a living? Besides, he'd never heard of a person in a wheelchair going to college and he wasn't eager to hear about it now.

He did suggest that, since I couldn't leave the house, I might consider typing envelopes at home. I could work at a very slow pace and not be bothered with other people around me — like what happens in offices. He added that sometimes people in wheelchairs had even been known to sell magazine subscriptions over the phone.

My parents and I stared at him in disbelief. I'd just finished high school, where I wasn't allowed to take typing because my wheelchair couldn't be accommodated in the classroom. My advisor had me take advanced chemistry, physics, math and foreign language because I obviously had to go to college if I were ever to learn a job skill that could be done from a wheelchair. Now the state was telling me I should have learned to type. And they thought I was the one who was confused.

Most universities couldn't accommodate anyone in a wheelchair even if their policies had permitted. The University of Wisconsin, with its campus built on hills, would have presented almost insurmountable barriers to getting to and from class. One slip and there would have been an excellent probability of flying down a hill and into Lake Mendota.

Then the swim coach, Jim Davies, remembered that a member of his swim team, who had polio at the same time I did, had gone to someplace called the University of Illinois in Champaign-Urbana. The rumors were that there was some kind of program through which people who used wheelchairs could enroll as regular students at the U of I. A number of calls to the university only revealed that no one we were able to contact had heard the rumor. Then, someone came up with the magic word — Tim Nugent.

Following World War II, Tim Nugent, who never seemed to mind that the rest of the world considered him certifiably insane, decided to prove that people with disabilities, of a severity level that permanently assigned them to using wheelchairs, could attend college on a basis equal to anyone else. In 1948, he had convinced the university to test this theory at a temporary division of the U of I located in Galesburg, Illinois.

As I was told the story by Tim and some of the guys who were the original guinea pigs, when the University closed Galesburg, they decided that was the end of the experiment. According to the legends, Tim led his gallant men down the streets of Springfield, the state capitol, and picketed the Governor's Mansion until the University relented and let 22 men and one woman, who used wheelchairs, onto the Champaign-Urbana campus. The number of original students didn't matter. The only fact we need to know is that students in wheelchairs were allowed to enroll on the main campus.

Further legend includes tales of Tim and his henchmen constructing ramps into class buildings — some versions place the construction at midnight by the light of the moon — and people in wheelchairs were suddenly on campus. Details of legends aside, the student rehabilitation program was established on the campus and was there when I needed it in 1957.

Getting into the program was a different story. U of I, the only university in the nation at the time that would accept students who used wheelchairs, couldn't accept the hundred or more prospective students who applied each year. Reportedly, Tim wasn't allowed to enroll any students other than the original ones. Then, in 1950-1951, there seemed to be a limit on how many students in wheelchairs could be on campus. Tim was pretty inventive on how he managed to keep within that limit. For example, if you didn't use a wheelchair all the time, you didn't count against his limit. And, Tim reasoned, he had a lot of us who only used our wheelchairs from the time we got up in the morning until we went to bed — and that certainly isn't a full 24 hours a day.

To get into the U of I, you had to get past Tim first. First, you had to catch him. For years, parents trying to enroll their offspring in the U of I often believed that Tim was a legend — like Paul Bunyon. Tim believed he was a legend. Instead of Babe, the Blue Ox, Tim had his military experience. Tim's "kids," some of whom were older than Tim, were often treated to his remembrances of escapades like escaping German forces by driving an army motorcycle under a team of Belgian horses. Or, the time when he was separated from his unit and captured an entire platoon accidentally while having a command of German consisting of the word "Scheiss." We never mentioned to him that serving directly under Eisenhower, Patton, Montgomery and MacArthur would have kept him busy switching theaters. He also claimed quite a number of army athletic and endurance records. We added them up once and decided he held the record for running 100 yards uphill, in full pack, carrying a man on his back, through mud while wearing snowshoes.

Finally, after my relentless mother ran Tim to ground and we succeeded in gaining an audience with him in Champaign, I found out that Tim didn't like me. He said I was spoiled. I didn't have the guts to stick with it and make it at the university. He listed the dozens of students, with better academic backgrounds than I, who had flunked out — in a semester or less. We slunk back to Wisconsin without hope. The letter of acceptance arrived the following week.

In the Fall of 1957, I went off to Champaign, entered the U of I and embarked on a love/hate relationship with Tim that's lasted nearly 40 years. It's been 99.9% love — .1% hate.

The .1% hate turned out to be the factor that made many of us succeed when all odds were against success. Tim was right. I wasn't ready for college (we still argue about the spoiled bit thirty years later). Tutoring hadn't quite prepared me for competition from students without disabilities, who had been groomed for Illinois from early grades. Socially, having missed out on teenage peer relations and adolescent experiences for all but a year and a half, I was probably equal to a seventh grader interacting with college students. Social life was complicated by the fact that, in 1957, many of the freshmen on campus had taken a detour to fight in Korea between high school and college.

Having rarely met anyone else in a wheelchair, I wasn't sure I liked people with disabilities. Some of them whined. Some were very sloppy. The Korean vets who'd been wounded in action scared the hell out of me.

Those of us with disabilities lived in any of the accessible dorms, but we were brought together while riding the lift-equipped buses or in the canteen or during other activities. Like all college students, the one thing we knew we had to get was an attitude — a philosophy. We romped through being outcasts of society, victims of cruel fate, the role of crusaders and the deserving of special favors. Sometimes we got through all these phases in a single Saturday afternoon.

Religion was sort of lumped in with philosophy and we reveled in swinging from Christianity to Judaism to Atheistic Existentialism with a few detours through Eastern philosophies. About all we ever decided was that there really is no rhyme nor reason to why one is disabled. And, none of us found any cures through religion or philosophy.

If I was socially unprepared for college, I was even less physically prepared.

After my parents left, I realized that I had never gotten in and out of bed by myself. I also had no legitimate plan of attack for using the bathtub either. I was pretty sure my dorm mates could tolerate me staying up all night, but would be less accepting of not entering the bathtub for a full semester. To make my life more miserable, the lift-equipped buses were being replaced that year. The old ones had been taken off to the junk yard. The new ones hadn't arrived yet.

Hostility is an excellent motivator. First of all, that damned Tim had predicted that I couldn't take care of myself and I was not going to let him be right so early in the game. Secondly, staying in my chair all night or letting a dorm mate I'd hardly met fish me out of the bathtub didn't seem the way to make friends in a hurry. I might have been able to push the mile to class — if I'd known where the class building was, so I'd better learn to get in and out of the station wagons that were substituted for the missing buses. At least, I reasoned, I did know how to get back in my chair from the floor in the event that my strategies for getting into bed or the car lacked some crucial details.

A couple of other girls in wheelchairs used the common bathroom. By peeking through the curtain, I was able to see that a straight chair beside the tub enabled them to crawl

21

out, then into their wheelchair. I dumped myself into the tub. "This is easy," I thought. "You going to be in there all night?" "I've got a date in 20 minutes." "Did you drown?" It was surprising how such a chorus of encouragement inspired me to slither out of the tub, onto the straight chair and into my wheelchair. I made a mental note that, next time, I'd put a towel on the seat of my wheelchair and avoid the exercise of peeling wet skin off vinyl.

Peer support was also a major help in getting into the station wagon the next morning. Chuck Elmer, the villain in the form of a physical therapist, was soothing. Leaning against the wagon with his arms folded, he gently encouraged us. "Get your ass in there. We haven't got all day." The older male students took bets on which girl's skirt would ride up the highest as she flung herself at the seat.

We had one week to prove to Tim — and ourselves — that we really were U of I material. We made it through that week.

Counseling on which classes to take was conducted by students in wheelchairs who had survived a year or more.

"You have to take physiology," Lola Lange told me.

"Why?" I asked.

"Because Tim wants us all to know enough about how our bodies work to be able to defend ourselves against doctors," she replied.

Lola decided five courses was a pretty good load for me. Four of the courses were good choices, but the only French course in an accessible building was advanced conversational French taught by a Parisian. Big D time occurred before I finally realized that what the teachers at Janesville Senior High consider speaking French and what Monsieur Whose-name-I've-forgotten considered speaking French were as similar as Chinese and Arabic.

When I was growing up, my sister and I had separate rooms. Our nearest little playmates were a mile away. Now I was living — 24 hours a day — with 500 other girls. Colleges should lock freshmen girls up in units of no more than four to a building. Dorm life was wonderful! Whole bunches of girls were around to talk, eat midnight snacks, compare the attributes of various boys. Some of these girls even studied. In Mattoon, Illinois and Janesville, Wisconsin, all the people you meet are pretty much alike. What a cultural revelation we had when our East Coast dorm mates unpacked dozens of cashmere sweaters. "You mean your father gives you anything if you threaten to cry?" one of my new friends from southern Illinois asked a Jewish girl from New York. "Mine would whomp me!"

Upperclassmen are the major source of education for the freshman girl. On any evening, the conversations might have included:

"How can you tell which men's houses are full of jerks?"

"Why don't any Italians or Irish live in Frat houses — only Greeks?"

"How can I hide my illegal corn popper in the closet? My roommate's clothes will catch fire."

"Does your mother really let you read books like this? Yeah, I guess, since she's in New York, she won't find out."

We also learned from the upperclassmen that the only time a respectable student starts to study for an exam is at 10:00 p.m. the night before. There were some great sunrises over old Lincoln Avenue Residence Hall.

By October, close friendships — and outright hatred —

had formed the dorm into groups. We roamed in packs of 8 to 15 girls. Outsiders to the pack were treated in the same fashion wolves treat a new arrival when food is scarce. My pack had three of us in wheelchairs. Donna was neat because she grew up on a farm and she was pretty and funny. Patsy was irresistible with the accent she'd learned growing up in Clover, South Carolina.

As the first semester continued, it became obvious that most of the girl-pack to which I belonged, being mostly upperclassmen, had something called a major. The major related to what you were going to do when you graduated from college. I'd never thought much about what I was going to do when I graduated from college because I'd never thought I'd go to college. The most input I'd had on my future had been from the Wisconsin Department of Rehabilitation — which, of course, knew that people in wheelchairs didn't do anything.

Although those of us who used wheelchairs lived in residences scattered across Illinois' huge campus, we frequently visited the student rehab center — SRC to all — where Tim and his staff usually hung out. Actually, as freshmen, we were supposed to visit the SRC on a regular basis — at least three times a week for "physical therapy." Physical therapy was Tim's answer to the requirement that all U of I students take physical education in addition to their other courses. Since many of us found a lot of things we'd rather do than lift weights or try out the parallel bars, Tim's staff spent as much time lurking in campus hangouts chasing strays as they did in any administrative or treatment activities.

It seemed logical to go to SRC to find out about majors. After all, Tim and his staff had come through with answers to questions.

Tim looked patiently at me and explained that I could be anything I wanted and added that girls in wheelchairs had often succeeded as executive secretaries or as vocational counselors, for example. U of I SRC was heavily supported by the Illinois Division of Vocational Rehabilitation. Illinois DVR head, Dr. E.C. Cline, may not have broken any rules to keep the program on the U of I campus going, but at Tim's insistence he certainly heated the regulations up and formed them in some pretty innovative directions. Illinois DVR, being somewhat ahead of the times, actually expected people with disabilities to get jobs when they exited the U of I. Since Illinois DVR had already seen success in these two areas for girls, they recommended those career paths highly. Never mind what state you came from. Tim worked with Illinois rules.

Tim, having known me for a few months, could not picture me as the ultimate secretary. He wasn't even sure he could picture me in a business office. "Take lots of psychology courses," he said.

I did. Introductory psychology wasn't much to my liking. Rats were something we shot in the tobacco shed back on the farm, not something we taught to push buttons to get food. I liked abnormal psych. The text book was full of all kinds of kinky stuff and the professor was a cute young blond who flirted with all of his female students including me. I was having big trouble seeing myself as a voc rehab counselor. I'd met two. The one in Wisconsin who wanted me to learn to type envelopes and Edan Nicholas, the counselor at SRC. Edan was cool. He'd had a brief career as a movie star and was rather talented as a baritone. When further roles in movies eluded him and when the demand for opera singers was pretty light, Edan chose to be a DVR counselor. He earned enough to live well while still starring in U of I musical productions.

Finally, Tim bluntly told me that, since I was only a freshman, I'd better concentrate my energy on becoming a sophomore. Before I could be anything when I grew up, I'd have to pass a lot of math, science and English courses.

"Besides," he grumbled, "all you kids in wheelchairs have been exposed to are hospitals and a few teachers. You don't even know about the outside world. Half of you went to special schools for disabled and you were so coddled that you don't even know how to compete in the real world."

Tim was right. Most of us hadn't had summer jobs to teach us about working. The kids whose parents had a business or profession knew a little bit about what Dad did. In those days, Mom was either a housewife, a secretary or a nurse. In my case, my experience would have led to being a county agricultural agent.

One thing I always hated was when Tim was right. Sure enough, as I thought about a career, I looked to the one experience I'd had other than farming. My roommate and several of my friends in the dorm were studying occupational therapy. What a neat thing to be! I could grow up to be like my beloved Miss Wolfgram, the physical therapist who become part of our family.

Occupational therapists, unlike physical therapists, didn't have to sling patients around. Instead, they did things like teaching crafts or helping people figure out what they could do to earn a living with what they had left after becoming disabled. O.T.'s worked in hospitals. That ought to be a good place for a person in a wheelchair to work. And the courses were fun. Judy, my roommate, and her fellow O.T. students, were taking much more interesting courses than me.

"I'm sorry, Jan," Edan said when I discussed it with him. "Students in wheelchairs aren't allowed to enroll in the O.T. curriculum."

"Why not?"

"The head of the O.T. curriculum — one of the finest O.T.'s in the country, I might add — doesn't believe in encouraging a person in an area where they couldn't succeed. For example, if you were teaching weaving, you couldn't use the foot controls on the loom. You wouldn't be able to climb ladders to get craft supplies. If a patient fell, you couldn't pick them up. And, if you worked in a psych hospital, you couldn't protect yourself against the patients. Even if she would let you into the curriculum, you have to finish your studies at the medical campus in Chicago — and there are no accessible buildings there."

Back to concentrating on surviving to be a sophomore.

chapter 4

College life before the era of physically challenged

The fact that most of the outside world considered people in wheelchairs as abnormal didn't filter into the close-knit world of my dorm. Looking back, it seems that life was a lot easier with a disability before all the organizations and agencies decided that people with disabilities were in need of special treatment. In those days at the U of I, you were pretty much considered to be in one or more categories used by students to classify people — nice/awful, smart/dumb, pretty/ugly, friend material/enemy material — that sort of thing.

Like when my roommate, Judy, greeted me with, "You'd better wash your hair and set it tonight. You're going to need to look good tomorrow night."

"Why? Did I win a blind date with a Sigma Xi?"

"Better. We chose you as our dorm's candidate for home-coming queen. You have to be at the auditorium at seven tomorrow night for judging."

University of Illinois founded the tradition of homecoming. On campus, homecoming outranked Christmas, Chanukah, Thanksgiving and Yom Kippur all rolled into one. But homecoming queens were not sex objects — if indeed that concept had even been invented in the late 50's. Illinois coeds were superior examples of young womanhood. Illinois may have been a land grant university — cow college to the Ivy League and eastern schools who looked down their nose — but Illinois coeds would be "finished" to the same degree as their Vassar sisters, if Illinois had anything to say.

The Deans of Women at Illinois had a lot to say. Associate Dean Eunice Dowse had achieved an outstanding high rank in the U.S. Navy before coming to Illinois. Associate Dean Mary Harrison, had similar high rank in the Army or Marines as had Dean Miriam Shelden. They ran the homecoming queen contest. The men students from the Greek houses or the men's dorms would not treat their young ladies lightly.

Equal opportunity for people with disabilities hadn't even been thought of, but Dean Harrison created it the night of the judging by declaring that, since I could not go up the steps to the stage and parade with the other girls, the whole event would be reorganized and we would all stroll down the aisle for review.

I didn't win the honor of homecoming queen — or one of the nine princesses representing our nine Big Ten rival schools, but the experience sure helped my self-esteem. Dean Harrison mentioned that, had I won, she would have enjoyed seeing how the pageant officials solved the problem of getting me on top of the stadium scoreboard for the half-time ceremonies.

At the end of my freshman year, Tim once more proved to have been right the preceding fall when he forecast that a lot of us wouldn't make it through our freshman year. Some of the kids in chairs hadn't made it past first semester. Most of the kids who had attended special schools for crippled children, as Tim predicted, didn't make it. "Those schools focus on disability more than subjects. They consider anything you do to be good — considering you're disabled," was the theme of one of Tim's favorite lectures.

My big D in French landed me on probation, but, if I had good grades the first semester of my sophomore year, U of I would welcome me to go on.

An influence that came into my life during my freshman year was named Marie Bevan. As head resident (the U of I term for house-mother, warden, whatever) of LAR South, Marie was different. The short, wiry redhead was only a few years older than her charges. She may have been a hellion hidden under her Mormon exterior because she reliably anticipated any type of trouble girls could find to amuse themselves. She was "Marie" to her girls. Other HR's were Miss Whoever. She knew which rooms had the illegal coffee pots and popcorn poppers and frequently helped herself to their products.

Marie and I became friends after I had visited the governing board several times. I never quite got the exact timing required to get in the door of the dorm before I was judged late. Three late offenses and you got to be judged by a jury of your peers. Usually, you were campused — couldn't go out on a weekend night.

Marie convinced me that my tendencies toward noncon-forming were probably a talent for leadership in disguise. Besides, she didn't have anyone else for the role of fresh-man advisor for the fall of my sophomore year.

Marie greeted me as I arrived back at LAR the fall of 1958 with, "Some of your dingbat freshmen are here early. Round them up and take them over to Illini Grove and tire them out at a picnic. I know you'll be back by closing be-cause you're an example for your freshmen."

None of my freshmen had ever known anyone in a wheel-chair. They apparently didn't have any ideas about how a person with a disability is different. They all chose to deal with the fact I used a wheelchair by not thinking any pro-found thoughts about the whole situation. They preferred such special treatment as, "Hey, Jan, I've got a really terrible exam to study for. Can you run down the street to the drug store and get some Kotex? I checked and you're all out — and you are supposed to be here for me aren't you?"

My dozen dingbats managed to survive freshman week, registration and even some classes. I lost one at Thanksgiv-ing when she persuaded her father that her homesickness outranked his desire to see his daughter graduate from his alma mater. I lost another when my patience — along with Marie's and that of the Student Health Service — wore thin coping with her suicide attempts. Overdosing on No-Doz kept her awake for two days. Overdosing on ExLax tied up the bathroom needed by the rest of the girls. Two more left at semester break with the advice from the university that perhaps they were more suited to life at a junior college.

It may have been that Marie was right that being responsi-ble for freshmen made me grow up or that I'd completed my language study requirements and didn't have to take any more damned French that made my grades improve in my sophomore year. More likely it was the fact that if I didn't make my grades, I couldn't be a Gizz Kid cheerleader.

chapter 5

The sports life

One of the things that I had liked most when I arrived as a freshman was the good old college spirit. As at most colleges, school spirit at Illinois was best expressed by supporting the school athletic teams. This was thrills beyond anything I'd known! The Marching Illini and Chief Illiniwek brought tears to my eyes. My dorm mates convinced me that wearing orange and blue underwear and singing the Illinois Fight Song in the bathtub were excessive behavior, but I'd never been part of anything like this before.

The guys and gals in chairs on the U of I campus had long felt the same. Guys who had been high school basketball stars before polio canceled their college scholarships, still wanted to live for the game. And so the Illinois Gizz Kids became the first college basketball team in the National Wheelchair Basketball Association. Actually, Tim and the Gizz Kids started the NWBA so they could compete.

In that era, girls played basketball in high school gym sometimes. Any girl who seriously considered competing in basketball — or most sports for that matter — was considered either a potential physical education teacher or a tomboy. Girls were cheerleaders. Girls in wheelchairs at Illinois could become cheerleaders if they survived the tryouts.

My ever-patient freshman roommate wasn't particularly surprised when I started practicing cheers. She did suggest there was more room to practice outside, but other than that was supportive.

"Why do you want to be a dumb thing like a cheerleader?" she asked. "Sports are for high school kids."

"Well," I replied. "I like sports and there aren't any that girls can be in, but being a cheerleader lets me go with the team — and I might see some place besides Champaign."

St. Louis, Kansas City, Cleveland, Nashville and Chattanooga certainly were some place besides Champaign. Since there were only 25 or 30 wheelchair teams in the country, the league in which U of I played had no teams closer than a four-hour drive away. The players on the other teams in our league, were working men, many of whom had been disabled in military service. They agreed to come to Champaign during the semester, when Gizz Kids couldn't get away from classes. For the men on the Kansas City and Chattanooga teams, it frequently meant leaving work early on Friday night, driving most of the night, playing Saturday night and driving most of Sunday to get back for the start of the work week. The St. Louis Rams had some financial support from the War Dads group, but most of the men paid their own way and drove their own cars to keep the league alive.

When semester break came, it was our turn to play on the other teams' courts. The guys on the other teams weren't crazy. Midwestern winters being what they are, the schedule let Illinois get to fight the blizzards in Kansas and the ice storms in Cleveland. For us Gizz Kids, this annual trek to battle was known as the "Tour." Going on Tour was sort of a tribal initiation rite. Those who were lucky enough to go on Tour were viewed with a certain awe by those who did not win that chance. To win the chance, you kept your grades up, gave up all of your free time to practice, surrendered your between-semester vacation and put up with Tim and Chuck Elmer at very close range — 24 hours a day for over a week.

Tim had experimented with taking the campus buses on Tour in earlier years. Since these buses were vehicles that had been retired from city bus service and were held together by wire and hope, the Illinois Gizz Kids had never made the full circuit of the cities that had to be covered on Tour — let alone make it back to Champaign. The old timers who lived through the days of Tour using the "Blue Bulls" buses captured the admiration of us youngsters by leaning back and saying things like, "Yeah! I was one of them that was marooned in Grinnell, Iowa for three days while we tried to find parts" or "being stranded in Cleveland wasn't bad. Fortunately, the gym floor we played on didn't collapse into the abandoned swimming pool until after the game."

Tim, having been embarrassed once too often by disrupting the schedule of the league he headed, decided to draw cars out of the University motor pool so we'd have a chance to keep on schedule. Of course, the logistics changed. Keeping five or six cars together proved challenging — but critical. Our luggage and our wheelchairs were in the only van in this motorcade.

Logistics were complicated by the fact that we frequently didn't know where we were staying at night until we arrived and found out what the host team had managed to arrange. If anyone knew where we were playing the night we arrived, it must have been revealed only to those with high security clearance. The drivers of the cars never seemed to be in that classification.

Being a part of the Tour built character. For us girls, it encouraged bladder control. We often had to wait for hours for potty stops because the guys could use tin cans and if the girls' car stopped, we might never find the rest of the cars. Staying in the caravan wasn't an art we ever accomplished. There was one memorable afternoon spent with half the team's cars going east-bound on a divided highway in Indianapolis until they spotted the other half of the team's cars going west-bound. East-bound would turn around at the first available cross-over — to find that west-bound had done the same and was now east-bound. This exercise was repeated several times before the driver/equipment manager/assistant coach managed a primitive, but effective, road block with his van.

We got so good at this maneuver we once spent nearly an hour going around the blocks on which the men's residence halls were located — two blocks from where we'd started — trying to get in line. We finally found Tim, who was arguing with the campus police that he was only going one way on the street and it wasn't his fault that the "One Way" sign was pointed in the other direction.

The games were not the total highlight of these trips. Getting there was truly half the fun. Using accommodations was 35% of the rest of the fun.

Very few of us had ever stayed in a hotel or motel. "Accessibility" in those days meant that the team could afford to stay in the flea bag. The cheerleaders shared rooms, cleverly choosing a roommate who could at least stand up and maybe even limp a little. That gave you someone to push the straight chair that you transferred onto from your wheelchair so you could get close enough to leap to the pot. Girls who could stand up could also reach light switches, get around the bed to the phone and other handy chores.

When we got in over our heads, our trusty chaperone came to our rescue. Dr. Echo Dell Pepper, who taught honors courses in calculus, bolean algebra and things like that at U of I, was a Scot, born and raised in Seattle. She frequently pointed out to us that it was incomprehensible to her why Midwesterners bragged about being able to see for miles in their states. There wasn't anything worth seeing in Dr. Pepper's opinion. At 4'10," weighing precisely 87 pounds and topped by a lot of auburn hair, Dr. Pepper gave her age as "somewhere near retirement."

But the 87 pounds was pure tiger. Dr. Pepper not only fulfilled the university requirements that women students must travel with a chaperone, she sewed up our torn seams, always had the right remedy in her bottomless carpet bag and taught us that it wasn't safe to drink the water. Proper young ladies never wore slacks, never went out in public without the proper underclothes — girdle and military-style bra — drank tea during the day and a glass of single malt scotch in the evening. What she lacked in strength, she made up in common sense. If you locked a suitcase rack open with a belt around the legs, it was a perfectly good way to get into a bathroom with a 22" door. The only problem Dr. Pepper ever caused was that everyone, including the guys, wanted her in their car and next to them at dinner.

A side benefit of going on Tour was what you learned. For example, in those days, the only curb cuts were occasional driveways. One Sunday morning in St. Louis, Tommy Joyce, Ron Stein and Bob Arnold declared that they were tired of helping me up curbs. Time to learn to jump up and down curbs. With two of them behind my chair and one in front, they tipped my chair back. "Keep pushing forward a little to keep the front wheels off the ground!" "Whoops! You pushed too hard!" as I plunged backward into the lap of one of them. With their encouragement — and the fact they stopped catching me in my backward moves — I soon was able to balance on the back wheels. The guys moved quickly on to practicing wheeling the chair while balanced on the back wheels. I learned that if you push fast enough, hit the curb with your back wheels and lean forward at the right time, you've jumped up a curb. Jumping down a curb was a simple matter of gravity and lack of concern about your neck.

Tour was probably more of an education for kids who had spent at least part of their lives being protected and cared for than the classrooms would ever offer. We found out that if you made enough racket, museums could always find an accessible path to the exhibits. So what if you rode with the paintings and junk on the freight elevator. A tram ride up a mountain near Chattanooga was just another adventure. Coaches carried those of us who couldn't walk to the tiny seats and the tram operator was so intrigued that he didn't charge for the ride. We found that those same coaches had no mercy if we decided to enjoy the nightlife of a particular city a little too late. One of Tim's rules was that the coaches had keys to all of our rooms in case of emergency. Not being ready to go in the morning counted as an emergency.

Some of us had never seen another young person in a wheelchair before coming to Illinois. On Tour, we found out that sometimes other people in wheelchairs are pretty interesting. Ron had been all-state in basketball when he had polio. Bruce had a tennis scholarship to U of I when he was hit with polio the summer before he was to enter college. Some of the Korean vets were bitter. Some of the team were accepting that they would always use wheelchairs. Between the lot of us, we worked out the idea that we'd better do what we could with what we had.

Flexibility was another thing we learned. Very few schools, colleges or other establishments wanted our wheelchairs gouging holes in their hardwood gym floors. A little carpet taped to the bottom of the footrests fixed that. We played in American Legion halls, National Guard armories and a few facilities that were probably intended for livestock auctions. If the facility had locker rooms, they weren't accessible. We learned that it was better to be cold than close the car windows and warm up our sweaty players on the trip back to the motel.

We thought we were hot stuff! We were the Illinois Gizz Kids, the most famous college wheelchair basketball team in the world — in addition to being the only one. The American public in the late '50's was less prepared for our onslaught on the world. It was not unusual for restaurant owners to rush to the front door and put up the Closed sign when they saw 15 or 20 orange and blue clad wheeled demons headed toward their establishment. One women's group, after we had invaded their town, wrote to the president of the University of Illinois and begged him to stop exploiting these young people in a freak show.

Educating the public was a challenge we attacked with glee — mixed with a healthy amount of sadism. We liked the effect when Dean Nosker told a woman who had patted him on the head and asked why he couldn't walk, "I washed my feet this morning and can't do a thing with them." We damned near sold tickets to the crowd who gathered to gawk at the sight of Bill Richards, who was born without arms, feeding Tom Linde, who had no control of his arms because of his cerebral palsy. Holding the fork between his toes, Bill took careful aim and stuffed the food in Tom's mouth. Another favorite activity was watching the reaction of ladies when Bill whipped out his lighter, flicked it on with his big toe and lit the lady's cigarette.

Competing for the most unusual answer to, "Why is a wonderful young person like you sentenced to a wheelchair?" — or variations thereof became as much of a sport as our basketball. We made up tales of tragic attacks by wild animals, incredible acts of bravery in which we became paralyzed and horrible misfortunes of war, that if the listener had paid attention, evidently occurred when the subject was 12. This activity was profitable. You could be rewarded by drinks, meals and, in one case, a proposal for marriage.

Groups of us in hotel lobbies were always good for our special game of "get the public." But, we were topped by a couple of very drunken men one night as we waited in the lobby across from La Guardia Airport. The two looked at us, sprawled on the furniture, our feet up in our wheelchairs. Then one dashed to the lobby screaming, "Call the fire department, call the police! There's been a hell of a crash and the bodies are all over the place — even wheelchairs!"

We fended off the offers of adoption, but enjoyed the friendships that grew with professional athletes. St. Louis Rams frequently scheduled our wheelchair games as part of the St. Louis NBA Hawks. I still have a slight crush on Bob Pettitt of the Hawks and Bob Cousey of the Celtics. Meadowlark Lemon totally blew us away when we met the Globe -trotters.

chapter 6

Career planning

Toward the end of my sophomore year, the question of what I was going to be when I grew up had to be seriously addressed. U of I doesn't let students wander through four years without a major.

If there were batteries of tests in those days that helped you decide what you wanted to be when you grew up, I missed them. The voc rehab counselors — if I'd had one — wanted you to go into something safe. Tim wanted you to be a raging success — preferably in an area all of the experts said couldn't be done by a person in a wheelchair.

I decided that I was an undiscovered journalist. I probably had never heard the term when I was a child. I just knew that I learned to read early and with practically no discrimination. When I asked for a particular book for Christmas, the clerk at the book store told Mother that this book was not reading matter for an eight-year-old. Mom continued to take pride in my precociousness until she opened a book I was reading when I was about 12 and got a full treatment of William Faulkner's best tales of incest and decadence.

The decision was reinforced by reality. The only courses I

liked in college were English, writing, math and science. Math was out. Differential equations and I could never share a lifetime. Only men became engineers so forget physics and chemistry. Teaching English interested me, but few school districts in the country allowed people in wheelchairs to teach. You couldn't reach the blackboard, climb the ladder to the supply cabinets and fend off attacks from the students, you know. Besides, it would have depressed the devil out of the little tykes to have a teacher in a wheelchair. But, U of I had a terrific school of journalism.

Journalism, which required a lot of physical work, might not seem a logical choice for a person in a wheelchair, but U of I journalism had already graduated several people in wheelchairs. Tim suggested medical technical writing.

However, the school of journalism at Illinois at that time was staffed by men who had earned their ways in the field. Dick Hildwein, who taught photography, had tramped around the world shooting for United Press International. Joe Sutton had been a newspaper editor. Glenn Hansen, who taught typography, not only could run a press, he was an accomplished artist in several areas of engraving. Ted Peterson and Wilbur Strang had based their textbooks on their real world experience. If I thought I could be a journalist, it was good enough for them. They simply taught you the ropes, not guaranteed success in the field.

John Schacht, my advisor, made an attempt to guide me toward medical technical writing, a field where there might be more opportunity. When I declared that I didn't think I was that kind of a journalist, he shrugged and told me that, as long as I could figure out how to handle the photo and typography labs and cover outside stories for reporting, it was my choice. Just don't try to take any of the "get and A without going to class" electives like public relations. The old street-wise guys in those days considered PR a sissy cop-out.

Journalism might never make me a living, I thought, but it changed me from a mediocre student to A-minus in one semester. Just entering Greg Hall, the class building where U of I confined the journalists lest they corrupt the other, more academic fields, made you feel part of the elite. The list of famous alums of the U of I journalism school was long. The fact that Hugh Hefner didn't really graduate did not exclude him from being claimed as one of U of I's great success stories. The fact that he kept the professors supplied with Playboy ties, passes to Playboy clubs, etc., didn't hurt.

Happily engrossed in the activities of journalism school, campus activities, the Gizz Kids and the dorm life, I flew through my junior and senior years. We seniors became restless our last semester. We wanted to go out into The Real World. After all, out there we wouldn't be sharing our private lives with 500 other girls — and we'd never ever have to be in by 10:30 p.m. On the other hand, we'd have to do something in the real world.

My roommates, Carol and Elaine, neither of whom were disabled, had their future all set. Elaine would marry Danny and go to England with him while he finished his hitch in the Air Force. Carol would marry Jack and begin her teaching career at University High in Urbana.

Quite a few of my female classmates in wheelchairs had achieved the ultimate goal of coeds in that era — engagement to be married. My adventures in finding a suitable mate had been less successful. While a number of students

44

who used wheelchairs fell in love and married others in wheelchairs, the love of my life, who used a wheelchair, and I came to a mutual decision. Two wheelchairs in one marriage were more than we could handle. Then there were guys who weren't in wheelchairs. One dropped out when he learned that his mother would disinherit him if he even seriously thought about taking on the burden of a crippled wife. Another exited when the law firm which he would join upon graduation pointed out that the role of wives in the firm was to be an impeccable social asset. Guess they wouldn't have accepted me too readily at the Junior League.

In short, my future after graduation was vague — actually, "unknown" was a more accurate label. The only employment potential that was solid was that I had scored high on the government service GSA exam. This score qualified me to work as a claims clerk at a social security office.

"It would be a very stable position." The counselor Tim had added to the staff to enable Edan to really work for Illinois, who paid him, was into stability. "You could stay with Social Security Administration until you retire," he added.

"I could have stayed in Janesville, Wisconsin and been a clerk for the county agent without having to struggle through four years of college," I replied. "The only difference is the county agent makes sure cows are registered properly and social security works with old people. I trained to be a journalist. I'm not going to spend the next 45 years of my life trying to catch old ladies cheating Social Security."

Graduation was impressive. Scotty Reston, one of U of I journalism's better known alumni said a lot of things about our challenges, our duties — the usual graduation speech.

Both Ron Stein and I were named as one of the top 100 U of I seniors. We sweated in our robes under the hot June sun in Memorial Stadium. Then we filed past our college deans and received a diploma cover that was empty. Diplomas would be mailed later.

If at first
you don't succeed —
you still have to
earn enough to live on

W e'd been spoiled by the U of I. We were treated just like everyone else on campus. Hadn't Ron and I even been chosen for top senior honors? The rest of the world wasn't as accepting. Neither of us "Top Seniors" were successful at finding a job right after graduation.

Tim didn't consider his responsibility for "his kids" to be over just because they'd graduated. Besides, he didn't consider letting any of us ruin his perfect record of all of his graduates finding a job. Tim had a lot of perfect records. Breaking them was not to be considered.

For example, Tim had a perfect record of never having anyone injured during wheelchair football. This game, invented by the high-spirited lads of the Gizz Kids, caused people to question Tim's claim that there had never been an injury. When the players battled at the university armory on Saturday mornings, it was not considered a completed play unless at least one player was knocked out of his chair — and preferably run over by an opponent. Uninitiated spectators cringed. I recall taking Gerald Jennings, the head of the world's largest wheelchair manufacturing company, to his first game. He started shaking when he saw the first spokes being ripped out of the wheels. He really had a bad time when one of the players managed to shear the wheel off an opponent's chair by the force of a head-on collision and the wheel sailed through the air and into the spectators. Nonetheless, Tim stood by his claim. One of the players noted that Tim would have buried you on the 50-yard line rather than admit to an injury. Besides, God gave you knuckles so you'd have some part of your body to get skinned.

Tim attacked the matter of two graduates without jobs in the same manner. With a quick bit of thinking and quicker budget magic, Tim performed the employment equivalent of memorializing a player on the 50-yard line.

Tim had a grant to develop standards for wheelchair accessibility which would become the basis of the first ANSI national code standards for buildings. Ron was the perfect person to supervise ramp pitches, door widths and turning radii.

My position set new records for Tim's creativity. By now, the limit of 90-125 handicapped students on the U of I campus was more in the range of 150+ — if you could have ever counted them all at one time. There was a lot of varied work needed to support student activities. I was given the title of assistant supervisor of special services and occupational therapy. The length of the title compensated for the depth of the salary. Adding OT gave credibility to the medical benefits to students that could be expected from state expenditures. If I had a job description, it was written on a magic slate and somebody pulled the cover up every day.

The student rehab program still was existing as an experiment — 13 years after the original start-up at Galesburg. It still was housed in the parade ground units (PGU). Expansion had been achieved by moving the student canteen into brand new quarters and letting SRC have half of a barracks adjacent to the original offices. For a program that wasn't quite authorized, had limited future, and was held together with string and stubbornness, the PGU's were perfect headquarters. The name, parade ground units, came from the fact that at one time, the University of Illinois had a crack cavalry unit and used the grounds for training horses and men. At the end of World War II, the cavalry unit was disbanded and the desperate need for housing for service men returning to college led the university to acquire tar-paper barracks at some remote military installation, truck them to Illinois and erect them on the old parade ground. Neither the trip nor the reconstruction improved the buildings.

When I first entered the university, the PGU's were still used for housing married students and some single men. The PGU's were perfect candidates for creating accessible housing for the men who used wheelchairs. They had sunk on their foundations so ramps didn't need to be steep. Doorways could be widened with a jack knife. In fact, one U of I legend is that Ray Nitschki, who went on to fame with the Green Bay Packers, created an exit in one of the units one night when he missed an intended tackle on a fellow occupant and left through the end of the building.

Decrepit is not a good word to describe the PGU's. But, there are no words in the English language to adequately explain their condition. When it snowed, drifts piled up on the floors near doors and where the walls might have met the foundations. SRC activities were frequently disrupted by falling acorns launched by squirrels who tried to bury them in what could have been the ceilings of the rooms. Some days the doors opened easily — and stayed open. Some days, the doors didn't open. It depended on which direction the building had sagged and whether the physical plant had gotten around to propping it back up.

In many ways, the building was a perfect match for the staff of the SRC which I joined. No one made much money. Tim could convince you that you ought to pay the university for the privilege of working there. We also didn't get paid on an often or routine basis. The program was always "falling through the cracks" or being moved from one budget, department or administration to another. If we'd had the money, the staff would have run a pool on which times we'd get paychecks. Tim told us that we were blazing a trail for disabled people everywhere. We were unique. Tim, we're broke. His reply to this was we were learning skills and attributes that would take us far in later life.

Probably, someone, somewhere in the administration had the idea that the term rehabilitation implied a medical orientation to the program. Actually, we did have the good Dr. Marion Kinzie. The jovial Dr. K spent as much of his time explaining that he not only hadn't written the current, world-famous study on sexual behavior, he preferred to leave that matter — and most other medical topics — up to the choice and ingenuity of the students.

True, Chuck Elmer was a registered physical therapist. He had even practiced in the air force. His unorthodox, but effective, method of treatment was to be such a pain in the ass that the students chose to keep fit enough to outrun Chuck and avoid him except when he was officiating at a wheelchair football game or partying.

Chuck was also the chief — and only — instructor in driver education. He may, indeed, have been the first in the country to instruct people to drive with hand controls. He approached this task with thoroughness — that's the steering wheel and that's the brake, you'll figure out the rest as we go along — patience and, probably, a good stiff belt before each session. Actually, he showed remarkable composure when I turned very wide on one of my first driving lessons and parked the car in a deep ditch that was, at the moment, filled with water. Chuck waded to shore and called a tow truck and turned my further instruction over to an unsuspecting new staff member. I wasn't sorry to lose him because it was making me nervous having him get out of the car at intersections, walk across and meet me on the other side if I made it.

Another example of Chuck's multiple talents was his excellence as a swimming coach. His tactics to inspire swimmers to excel probably wasn't something the NCAA ever approved, but they worked. For example, after I almost drowned myself trying to finish a Class I race, much too long for my skills, Chuck decided I should swim as a Class IA, the new NWAA division for quadriplegics. It wasn't based so much on the fact that I was a quadriplegic, but more on the fact that we'd just gained some super Class I women swimmers on the Gizz Kid team.

"You're swimming breaststroke, freestyle and backstroke at the meet next week," he informed me.

"Chuck," I explained, "you remember that I can't keep my head out of the water far enough to inhale anything but water when I do the backstroke and I can't cough enough to exhale the water when I'm on my back. Besides, my left arm is so much stronger than my right that I swim in a circle until I drown."

Unfortunately, this discussion took place while I was resting, holding on to the end of the pool. Chuck stepped on my fingers with one foot and put the other on my forehead and shoved. It immediately dawned on me that a double overhead stroke was good. Chuck relented and let me wear a nose clip to lessen the flow of water into my head and I went on to set international records for that stroke. Chuck was good at knowing when someone just needed a little extra encouragement and confidence building.

His resourcefulness wasn't limited to campus. One time, when the team was in New York, Chuck and I decided to explore the nightlife of the Bronx. When it became inevitable that I could no longer ignore the need to use a restroom and that there was no accessible restroom — possibly in the entire borough — Chuck borrowed a dime, dropped it in the jukebox, gathered me up in his arms and danced me into the restroom. Depositing me on the stool, he departed, telling me to scream when I was ready to come out. We figured no one would be unduly alarmed by a scream in a bar in the Bronx.

Tim strengthened the illusion of medical aspects of the SRC when he hired Gibb Fink as an occupational therapist.

Gibb's approach to occupational therapy made Chuck's unorthodox practice of physical therapy look anemic. Like Chuck, Gibb was a registered therapist. He'd even practiced at a large mental institution in Illinois. Those of us who got to know him were always pretty sure that the administration of that facility had a difficult time distinguishing Gibb's behavior from that of the paying guests.

The term "free-spirit" was a start — inadequate to be sure — in describing Gibb. He tore madly about campus in the rain with an umbrella mounted on his head. When Tim told him to make the place presentable for a visit from prospective donors, Gibb framed Tim's picture with a toilet seat. To get the point across to the U of I physical plant that the ceilings in the PGU's weren't up to standard, Gibb installed papier mache squirrels peeping through holes above our heads.

Gibb's talents were endless. He could weld, run a photo darkroom, build a house, fix a bus — show it to him and he'd fix it. His favorite activity, however, was creating havoc. We once lost track of him in Madame Tussard's Wax Museum, but knew we'd found him when we saw a crowd gasping and arguing in front of one of the displays. Gibb had sat down and put his arm around one of the female wax figures. At intervals, he'd wink or stick out his tongue in a very good impersonation of a wax figure coming to life.

With no legitimate funding to keep activities of the disabled students on campus organized, we improvised. Whoever had previously owned our mimeograph machine probably got a new one before it appeared in our office shack.

Newsletters were an important thing in reaching the students scattered across campus. Aligning stacks of sheets to be stapled was boring. Gibb invented a device to shake the collated sheets into alignment. By hanging a three-sided box from a chain hooked to the ceiling and attaching a 1/2 h.p. motor with an offset weight to the box, the creation vibrated well enough to shake a phone book into alignment. Unfortunately, there was a design flaw. As it vibrated, the box began to describe an arc which grew into a circle which continued to gain momentum until the whole apparatus reached head-height and resembled a one-bladed helicopter. It was a brave — or absent-minded — man who would charge in and un-plug the unit to halt its flight.

Which introduces Stanley Labanowich. Actually, Stan joined us as director of recreation and athletics after Casey Clarke went on to greater challenges like the U.S. Olympic Committee. He played a key role not only in the coming of age of wheelchair sports at U of I, but on the national and international scene as well. Casey was one of the most orga-nized, efficient people I ever worked with. Stan could make a star athlete out of the most unlikely person. But, being part of the SRC staff, he had to have some eccentricities. He brought a nice measure of absent-mindedness to the crew.

There were the small things — like always forgetting to put the cap on the ink supply for the mimeograph machine, but the black spatter pattern on the walls added to the decor. He forgot to buy a new battery for his ancient Austin auto which meant that, more often than not, he had to use the crank to start the car. For those who don't remember that cars could be started by sticking a crank into some recepta-cle at the front of the car, you are unaware that cranking a car to start it ranked right up there with teasing fighting bulls and falling off roofs on the scale of unsafe activities. Finally, Gibb, fearing for the lives of Stan and the surrounding citi-

54

zens, stole the crank, dug a hole in the ground and buried the dead battery to help Stan remember to buy a new one.

His habit of driving his car to track practice, then taking the team bus back to the SRC was an indication Stan concentrated on his athletes. His ever-patient wife, when he called to ask her to pick him up, would explain that, since the car wasn't in the driveway, he'd driven it to work. Please ask the track team members to suggest where he'd left it.

Although wheelchair sports were a crucial factor in helping many of us with disabilities develop the independence, competitive nature and other traits that launched us into fuller lives, there was less money to conduct wheelchair sports than there was for education. That meant a permanent deficit budget. Enter on the scene the United States Air Force to the rescue.

Chanute Air Force Base, in Rantoul, Illinois, a few miles from the university, not only was our source for certified officials for wheelchair basketball and football contests but came through when the National Wheelchair Basketball Association spread across the nation and there seemed no way for teams to pay their way to the annual tournament. Tim and one of the rehab programs angels. Seeley Johnston, approached General Byron E. Gates, commander at Chanute. General Gates liked the idea. In 1955, Chanute provided the gym, barracks to house the players and a great Non-Com officers club for parties. For the next five years, General Gates and, later, General Hopwood, made it possible for NWBA teams to fly to tournaments held at Air Force bases. An Illinois Senator brought Air Force transportation to a halt when the Gizz Kids had to travel to El Toro Marine Base in California to defend their national title. But, Senator Douglas had only told congress the air force couldn't fly civilians. he forgot the navy, who happened to route a plane to El Toro through Chanute at midnight — and newspaper and TV people just happened to be driving by the base.

In fact, two key players on the SRC — by now, the Division of Rehabilitation-Education services — staff who made higher education possible for people with disabilities had retired from Chanute after completing 20 years of service.

Henry Bowman, a member of the first Black Air Force unit, passed through SRC service before going on to break barriers for blacks in areas including NCAA officiating and U of I executive ranks and ending up as a vice president of personnel for Hilton Corporation. Hank used the fact that every student in a wheelchair admired his wit and sophisticated manners as an opportunity to put the idea in our minds that education, impeccable speech and manners, and good appearance can make people momentarily forget about the fact you're different. Actually, he said things like, "Just because you're a gimp doesn't mean you have to look like a rolling rag bag" and "a lot of success comes from being the right nigger in the right place at the right time," which, of course, would never had flown in the politically correct eras that came later.

Bob Wright, the other air force retiree, was the model for a TV program called "Sergeant Bilko." Wright was in charge of keeping the campus buses running, making sure we had athletic equipment and remodeling university regulations, when needed, to fit the situation. Wright taught us things like how to tell good scotch from rotgut and said things like, "Kiss what and go where?" and "take two, buddy, and hit the left." We never quite figured out what he meant, but he was a sure bet to scare off do-gooders.

The staff wasn't totally male. There was my buddy, Louise Fortman Jones, whose job was to try to keep Stan from disappearing in stacks of paper or team uniforms, make sure that he got to the games he was coaching and other little things. When I saw Louise for the first time at freshmen orientation when we both entered U of I, I hoped I wouldn't like her. How could you like a girl who looked like Kim Novak, sitting in a wheelchair just for kicks, and with a sense of humor that couldn't be ignored.

Since the SRC was the closest thing existing to a coordinating factor for students with disabilities on campus, a variety of high-spirited, creative and frequently down right nasty students were in and out daily. Most of them had disabilities. Since it would take another 20 years after the first severely disabled people went out into the ordinary world to form stereotypes about what disabled people are like, the discrimination they face and the other facts social scientists have worked out, we were able to move rather smoothly toward progress.

chapter 8

The first independent living experiment

In the years of progress for the disabled that followed, a lot has been done about campus programs to provide college experience for people incapable of handling their own daily living activities. Many of these programs have been the result of extensive studies, government grants and social movements. In 1961, Tim decided that there still were people whose disabilities prevented them from enrolling in U of I. It took him less than two months to start the new program.

To go to U of I, a student with a disability had to be able to be physically independent without the use of an attendant. And relying on your roommate wasn't allowed either. Still, promising students who could not meet those criteria were applying.

Tim was convinced that these people had been let down by the chicken outfits that called themselves major rehabilitation facilities and that, given the proper opportunities and incentives, these people could learn to become self-sufficient. Never one to muddy the water with things like opinions from medical experts or proposals for new projects, Tim just leaned on the U of I housing administration to allow us to use parts of the men's dorms a week before official opening and invited a few prospective students to attend functional training week.

"Congratulations, Jan," Chuck said as I went into my office one morning in late August. "You've won an all expenses paid week in scenic Garner Hall."

"Hey! I've finally got my own apartment — which I see only in the dark as it is. Why would I want to move to Garner?"

"Change builds character. Go home and pack what you'll need for a week and be back by six. Your first ones arrive tonight."

"My first what?"

"You get to guide five young ladies into total independence over the next week. I'll be across the breeze way with six guys," Chuck continued. "We've got a nice mix of quadriplegics and CP's. None of them can get in or out of bed without help."

"Chuck, damn it! Have you ever noticed that I'm a quad. How am I supposed to handle five girls who can't even blow their own noses?"

"One look at you will probably motivate them to be more creative than they ever heard of — you'll think of something."

Small talk and some food helped Gerry and Char — and me — overcome the panicked thoughts of how we were going to make it to morning. We decided that we would not tackle showers at all that night — just a quick wash up, then on to Topic One - The Advantages of Sleeping in a Bed over

Spending the Night in our Wheelchair.

Gerry was first. Her disability made it very hard to bend her limbs and her movements were slow to the point of not being noticeable. She was smaller than I, though, so with a great deal of slow bending, slow moving and strategic pushes, we soon had one graduate in the bed entering class.

Char, however, was a bit larger than I with the wet-spaghetti muscle tone typical of people who had a thorough case of polio. Together, we inched her chair up to the side of the bed — lift one foot onto bed, lift other foot onto bed. Move feet forward. Move wheelchair forward. Reasoning that if we could somewhat control a forward fall, Char would mostly land in the bed, I got on the bed and pulled. Most of her landed as planned. I pushed the rest of her in as we both giggled uncontrollably. She was asleep before I finished throwing a blanket over her.

By starting at 5:30 the next morning, both girls and I were in wheelchairs and decently covered with clothing by the time Chuck came in at 7:30. Gerry and Char looked a little glazed when he cheerily pointed out the canteen half a block away and assured them that pushing there would help them work up an appetite.

"Give me some money," I told Chuck.

"Why?"

"If I'm going to get people into bed half an inch at a time, I'm at least going to buy some slippery sheets for the bed."

The two girls and the nine other functional trainees who joined them that day weren't in any danger of not burning up every calorie they ate at breakfast. Chuck worked on teaching them how to get on and off the bus lifts, timing them to see if they could push from the bus stop to their class in a 20 minute time and instilling in them that being able to push yourself wherever you had to go was a virtue that would ensure your entry into Nirvana — or at least the U of I. Gibb worked in his "gadgets-and-gimmicks-make-you-free" mode. For Char, he made a rope ladder that let her pull herself into a position to start getting out of bed. Others had buttons on clothing replaced with Velcro™, fancy hand splints replaced with rubber bands to hold a fork and other unlikely, but effective, ways to do what they had to do.

There were a few glitches in some of the original designs, like the pull-tabs he made to enable Jane to remove the cap from her urinal leg bag so she could empty it independently. It stuck until I leaned close to see what was wrong. Then it came off, drenching me with the contents of the leg bag. "I've always heard the expression 'Piss on you,' Little," Gibb howled as I raced to the shower. "Now I've seen it — even funnier than it sounds!"

Necessity — or the prospect of "flunking" functional training — worked with this group. By Thursday, Char had cut 45 minutes off the time it took her to get out of bed. Gerry had mastered all the distance pushing. Eve had worked out a way to arrange her long hair and put on make-up and Jane drained her leg bag reliably without soaking me. There was no need to mention bed time. Gals and guys alike dropped into bed as soon as Chuck and I stopped harassing them.

I had just showered and was heading over to another men's dorm to share some probably illegal beverages when I heard shouting from a group of very drunken fraternity rushees, returning to their temporary quarters in Garner Hall.

"Hey! There's a bunch of crippled freaks staying in the rooms on the first floor."

"Let's scare the hell out of 'em. What are they doing here anyway?"

As the hope-to-soon-be frat rats ran up and down the corridor, pounding on doors, I realized that Chuck and Gibb had both gone off to other duties. I almost got the door to the girls' side of the dorm locked when two of the frat rats grabbed my chair.

"Can that thing go down steps?" they giggled. "Let's see if you fly." It wasn't going to kill me — but it was going to hurt a lot. But their racket had produced another force. It had awakened — and angered — the U of I Fighting Illini housed on the second floor. Team members rushed down the stairs, decided that this unscheduled scrimmage looked like fun and started tackling, cracking heads and terrorizing. There may be, somewhere in this country, a former Illinois frat member who could claim he was used as a tackling dummy by Archie Sutton or Dick Butkus — or maybe used for passing practice by Jim Grabowski or Fred Custardo. It was a short, one-sided episode.

All but one of our trainees registered for their classes the next week. It's too bad the experiment wasn't funded by a government grant because the tax payers would have gotten their money's worth. Out of the group came two college professors, a leader in the profession of speech/language pathology, a couple of business people and the heads of some fine families.

Functional Training Week was immortalized by one of the participants in a ballad, some of the words, set to the tune of Allen Sherman's "Camp Grenada" which went as follows:

"Hello Mother — so how are ya,
Please don't let this letter jar ya,
College will be entertaining
If I manage to survive functional training.
I tried prune juice
What disaster
And I lost my right front caster
And a speeding bike just hit me.
Please, oh, please let me come back
To New York City."

The author, Saul Morse, not only didn't go back to New York City, he became a lawyer and an active player in Illinois government. He also has spent the intervening years trying to make people forget he wrote the ballad.

Any student of literature knows that comedy is the flip side of tragedy. That's why theater is symbolized by the funny two-faced mask — one side laughing, the other, crying. Maybe it was because we were so into poverty that we had to make our own entertainment. Maybe it was because the students and staff connected to the SRC were so sick of pity and tragedy that they reacted by laughing.

In the decade of the '60's, the field of rehabilitation medicine was still struggling to be recognized as a significant medical discipline. For the next three decades, rehabilitation medicine would develop into an extensive field, but it would emerge as a paternalistic structure. Although the medical professionals who cared for the disabled frequently expressed themselves as having a mission to help people with disabilities, those same attitudes often meant that the person with the disability was trapped in the role of an individual who needed to have others decide what was best for them.

Very few of the disabled students at U of I had been subjected to the new methods of treatment and those who had been, chose to escape. Others of us hadn't been through rehab so we didn't know that we couldn't be our own person. If the able-bodied members of the SRC staff had a mission, it was to survive on no pay long enough to get a degree and a decent paying job. They didn't have time to distinguish between how they differed from guys and gals who happened to use a wheelchair or staggered a lot when they walked. This led to a lot of creativity in free entertainment.

Fun was a lot easier in those days. If you'd used the term "politically correct," whoever you were talking to would probably think it referred to whether you'd registered to vote — or that you supported the same party as your parents had. Being unencumbered with having to be PC, we entertained ourselves by making fun of each other.

Louise and I thought it was pretty amusing when we got Gibb and Chuck embarrassed in front of the College of Physical Education. Since these two were being paid as assistant professors, the U of I suggested that they teach a course. They chose kinesiology for occupation therapy students. First, the class was all girls. Second, kinesiology was a pretty vaguely defined topic at that time. Louise and I dressed Stan and Tommy, one of the grad assistants, up as visiting dignitaries, who happened to be medical missionaries and sent them to the class. Chuck and Gibb used the impending visit to tell anyone who would listen how important their course was — after all, these experts were coming from Spain! Then Louise and I sat back and watched as Gibb and Chuck tried to explain to the dean of the college that they'd been the victims, not the perpetrators, of the farce.

Staff members were the favorite material for students practicing their talent in satire, in addition to practical jokes.

It gets cold and snowy in Champaign in the winter and more time spent inside — like at the campus canteen — gave students the time needed to develop the theme for a holiday bash. It started small with one of the students writing words to the tune of "Davey Crockett" that declared Tim had been born in a brewery in Milwaukee, drunkenest state in the land of the free and been rehabilitated when he was only three. The refrain ended with the line, "Timmy, Timmy Nugent, King of the DAB." The acronym, it was pointed out, stood for Dead Assed Bastards.

When roasting individual staff members lost some challenge, the students took on the whole rehabilitation/disability profession. Spearheaded by Bill DeLoach, who had severed his spinal cord in the cervical area when he was a seminarian and who went on to become a professor in Tennessee, the group re-wrote "My Fair Lady." It came out "My Chair Lady." Some of the hit songs were, "I've Grown Accustomed to Her Brace," a number which pointed out that Chuck enjoyed the cries and moans of those who absent-mindedly went to physical therapy. "Get Me to the Class on Time" commented on the unreliability of the campus buses. "I'm Getting Married in the Morning" became "I'm Giving Counseling in the Morning" and roasted the counselor of the moment. Liza Dolittle, portrayed by a tiny, cute redhead, plaintively sang that "all I want is an old folks home — just a place to be all alone" where she would never have to learn to transfer or do anything for herself. Her other big number was "Just You Wait, Timmy Nugent, Just You Wait." And, of course, a student, portraying Tim in the role of Henry Higgins, rushed about the stage singing, "why can't the experts learn to rehabilitate — this pseudo branch of medicine is in a hopeless state."

Tim liked the production so much that he immediately arranged for the troupe to be the entertainment at the annual conference of the Easter Seal Society in Chicago the following spring. Since there was no noticeable distinction between which people were students and which were staff, we joined forces to make this presentation even better.

When wheelchairs wore out or were unsuitable for use on the campus, they were never thrown away. They went into Gibb's pile of "good stuff" that cluttered about a quarter of the space in one of our tarpaper shacks. Bob Wright and Gibb also added "good stuff" that Chanute AFB had discarded to the pile. For a while, we owned parts for the braking mechanism of an air force jet. The two midnight requisitioners figured it might come in handy for something.

The pile of "good stuff" was the inspiration for a line of wheelchairs designed to do what students really needed — not just transportation. The Cherry Picker was a seat mounted six feet above the wheeled base and driven by a long chain drive to the front wheel. This chair, they reasoned, would open new employment opportunities to the disabled. They could become migrant fruit pickers or life guards. Another chair was a bed — complete with head board, book shelves and reading lamp — aimed at the student who was too lazy to get out of bed before going to class.

Student protests were just emerging. The experience of some of the disabled students who had engaged in such protests was that it was impossible to go limp in order to force the police to exert extra effort in loading them into paddy wagons. The chair designed to meet this need disintegrated into pieces when the student pulled a lever. To allow equal participation in current dances — such as the twist and the Watusi — Gibb mounted eccentric, oval shaped wheels on a chair. This resulted in as much up and down as forward motion. For students who wanted equality in dating, there was the love seat. One chair was mounted facing a second chair with a common wheel between them. There was even a window shade that could be pulled down for privacy when necking progressed to petting.

The favorite chair of most of the students, however, was the ultimate solution to inaccessible bathrooms. This model featured a cardboard replica of an old-fashioned outdoor toilet mounted on the chair. Holes in the side of the structure allowed the occupant to reach out and wheel the chair down the street.

With the completion of the new line of wheelchairs, we were ready to head for Chicago and entertain the folks attending the National Easter Seal conference. Not only would this give us the chance to carouse in Chicago Loop night spots, it would provide us with a captive audience of a class of people we had a message for — executives of charities focusing on people with disabilities. The outbursts against Jerry Lewis from people with muscular dystrophy, coming to the forefront in the '90's, have a long history. If you have a disability, you can develop some animosities toward people who make their living raising money by playing on pity.

The average person, watching a telethon or reading an appeal, has an "oh, how awful for a kid to be crippled (thank god it's not me)" and "I wish I could do something" reaction. "Ah, but you can help!" the charity assures them. "Send money and you'll feel warm and fuzzy." Some of this money goes for research. In the case of the modern-day Easter Seal, it goes to support treatment centers that are truly helpful to children. But, most of us, then at the U of I, had been more hurt than helped by charities. The March of Dimes — famous for the little kid staggering on crutches, a feat made possible only by the dimes you, dear contributor, sent — used their funds to send employees on junkets. Families of kids like me who had polio were told that there was no help for individuals. Those of us with disabilities strongly suspected that charities caused two problems for us. People who gave to the charity felt they'd done their part and they'd rather not deal with us as employees or neighbors. The general public had a hard time separating the cute little crippled kid image from the reality of a capable, competitive adult with a disability.

The fancy dinner party that was the culmination of the conference was lovely— huge hotel ballroom, decorated exquisitely — hundreds of beautifully dressed people in the audience applauding the officials, who were, of course seated on the stage under larger than life photos of little crippled kids struggling on crutches. Our group had enjoyed the dinner. We weren't allowed to eat in the dining room with the benefactors, but us beneficiaries didn't mind.

The dinner guests were probably fortifying themselves to endure a bunch of cripples being pushed on stage to sing off-key when they ordered their after-dinner drinks. For what seemed a very long time, no one laughed as producer/director Bill DeLoach prompted his players in the re-write of "My Fair Lady." The audience probably really believed the first song "All I Want is an Old Folks' Home" expressed the true feelings of the cute little girl in a wheelchair who sang it. There was some nervous laughter from time to time, but the audience didn't seem to get into the act.

Undaunted by the lack of a standing ovation — or much more than some half-hearted applause, we launched our presentation of wheelchairs as they should be. That went pretty well. Stan and I managed to get the love-seat all the way across the ballroom despite the fact we never did agree which one was steering the craft. Gibb brought gasps from the ladies and genuine laughter from the gentlemen when he lost control of the outhouse chair and leaped out, clad only in his Fruit of the Looms to chase the roll of toilet paper. The show had a crashing finale. Stan got too confident in the Cherry Picker and turned too quickly, which caused the chain drive to jump off the steering wheel. Stanley landed in the middle of a table, wiping out the floral arrangement, eight after-dinner drinks and the decorum of the guests.

chapter 9

Never look
a gift bus in the mouth

We didn't mind starving in musical comedy. Our real opportunities for success lay in the field of athletics. By now, wheelchair sports had grown beyond basketball and our goal was to get to New York and win medals for Illinois in track, field, swimming, table tennis, weightlifting and the other sports sanctioned by the National Wheelchair Athletic Association.

Getting to New York presented a challenge. Tim either didn't learn from past experiences, or was blindly optimistic. Through the years, Tim had earned loyalty from a diverse assortment of business people. One of these supporters, Carmont Blitz, owned a company in Chicago that maintained and repaired the buses for Greyhound. Somehow, Carmie found a bus that had earned the right to the automotive equivalent to being put out to pasture after long service. It was put out to pasture by being donated to the U of I. Carmie was good. By the time he got done, that bus looked like it still had some years of service in it.

Tim wanted it to look better. After all, we were the only university wheelchair sports team that had its own bus. Always the competitive soul, Tim announced to the officials who ran the games in New York that, not only would Illinois storm into town on their own bus, he'd provide transportation for all competitors between event venues.

The whole city of New York was going to know that the University of Illinois was an important player in the national games. That bus would shout "Illinois." At the last minute, Tim realized that the people riding inside the bus couldn't see the two foot high "University of Illinois" painted in orange and blue on the bus sides.

"Gibb — you and Jan can make slip covers for the seats that say 'Illinois Gizz Kids' on the front and back," Tim told us about a day before we were to depart. Frantic silk screening operation. Frantic antics with the sewing machine. The day of departure dawned and each of the over 30 seats on the bus were wearing slip covers emblazoned with "Illinois Gizz Kids."

"Hey, you guys in the last four rows — don't lean back 'til we're through Indiana!" Gibb shouted. "The ink ain't quite dry."

With the lower storage areas packed with bows and arrows, javelins, endless bags of uniforms and a few suitcases and wheelchairs, we took off. By the time we hit Indiana, not only were the guys in the last four rows not leaning back, everyone was leaning ahead. In addition, a lot of us were holding our breath for long periods.

Shortly after we crossed the Illinois-Indiana state line, Freddy, who was driving at the time, remarked to Don, the senior driver, that the bus seemed to lurch and lunge no mat-

71

ter how steady he held the accelerator. The lurching and lunging was shortly accompanied by loud grinding noises. Don and Bob Wright decided to pull off at the next service plaza in Elkhart.

It didn't take Don and Bob long to discover that most of the oil from the transmission was now covering Interstate 80-90. The repairman at the service plaza was polite and concerned.

"Reckon I got no tools to work on something this size. Don't hardly ever see buses need fixin' here. Course, I wouldn't have the parts. Probably can get them in Toledo — maybe Cleveland."

"Can you do anything?" Wright asked.

"Sure, we can get her set in gear and you can run her. You keep checking the oil in every once in a while, and you can probably nurse her to Toledo — maybe Cleveland."

"Great!" Wright growled. "I can see us stopping every 10-15 miles to put more oil in."

"I wouldn't stop her, if I were you," our mechanic friend advised. "Probably never get her to go again. Keep her running."

I don't recall the mechanical details — probably didn't understand them at the time — but between Bob, Don and Gibb, a system was worked out by which, at appropriate intervals, Bob and Don would hold Gibb's feet and he'd lean out to check whatever he could see. He'd had experience with the Blue Bulls, so he became bus doctor.

As the morning wore on, it was apparent that the treatment wasn't curing the problem — maybe not even delaying disaster very effectively. Freddy asked Don to light a cigarette for him and put it in his mouth. We then realized that

Freddy was convinced that if he took either hand off the wheel, the entire bus might explode — or leap off the side of the earth or something of that magnitude.

"We don't stop 'til Toledo!" Wright commanded in his best air force officer manner.

"Not even for that toll booth coming up?" we chorused.

That bunch never failed to find a quick solution. No problem. After all, Chuck was following us in a car he was driving back east for one of the girls on the team. Chuck could dash ahead, pay the toll and tell the toll booth attendant that we wouldn't be stopping. The guys held a sign up in the bus' back window. "Chuck. Can't shift down. Pay toll. Clear booth."

Chuck responded by pulling along side and yelling, "I don't have enough money to pay your toll!"

We shook our change. The guys dangled Don through the window and most of the money landed on the seat of the car Chuck was driving.

Chuck handled the first two toll gates. Shoving money in the hands of the toll gate attendant, he shouted, "Bus. Can't stop. Full of people in wheelchairs!" Startled, the attendants cleared the gates and we sailed through.

Evidently, the second toll gate attendant re-thought the episode as we disappeared down the road. As we approached the gate at Maumee, Ohio, the road was cluttered with flashing lights. "Wow!" we yelled. "There's the Ohio state police — that looks like sheriffs' cars — maybe the Ohio National Guard is here, too!"

Whoever was in attendance was convincing evidence that we had to stop. Reluctantly, Don helped Freddy bring the bus to a halt. The bus gave a couple of belches of black smoke. Those team members who could, limped off the bus and a couple of team managers started pulling wheelchairs out of the storage areas. An Ohio state trooper threw his Smokey Bear hat on the ground — hard — when a reporter showed up to record the apprehension of a dangerous band of disabled athletes.

We won more medals than any other team at that year's national games.

chapter 10

See the world today — in your E & J

In keeping with their habit of using any music they heard for parody, the Illinois Gizz Kids had re-worded a ubiquitous General Motors ad from "See the USA — in your Chevrolet" to "see the USA in your E & J" — the brand of wheelchair used by everyone in those days. In the spring of 1962, the "USA" in the jingle was changed to "world."

Wheelchair sports had begun in England at about the same time they started in the U.S. and had become widespread in other European countries as veterans of various wars sought to restore their lives. Several of our men from the Gizz Kids had been chosen for the first USA Paralympic team and had competed in Rome, Italy in 1960.

Our U of I women's Gizz Kid team was a solid contender. The orange and blue wasn't a welcome sight at the national games in New York as Ella Cox, Hope Chaffee, Joanna Cornett, Alberta Richetelle, Evelyn Mulry and others took the titles in their classes in swimming, track and field. I failed to make the field team in Class A —there was no Class IA competition in field at the time — when my efforts in putting the shot landed reliably on Tommy's toe as he stood beside my chair. Jack Whitman had managed to make enough of an archer of me that I could usually place in the medals.

In early '62, rumors started circulating that we'd be heading for Africa. A man named Tom Knowles, a travel agent in Grahamstown, South Africa, was a paraplegic. The attitude of the public in South Africa toward people with disabilities annoyed Tom. He was determined to educate the public that people with disabilities were strong, capable, active individuals. His friend, John Powell, had left Rhodes University in Grahamstown to teach at the U of I. When John told Tom about the Illinois Gizz Kids, Tom decided that running the Gizz Kids around South Africa would be a great way to call attention to the abilities of people who'd crashed cars, had polio or in other ways qualified to use a wheelchair for the rest of their lives.

Tim chose the people who would be on the team. The process was mysterious and unknown to those of us who were chosen. The rules were that every member had to be a college graduate and employed. Tim made sure the team members were chosen for diversity and character — and he came up with a bunch of diverse characters. They came up with a bunch of diverse characters. Fourteen men and four women representing a cross section of geographic origin, occupation and disabilities would make up the team which would demonstrate sports, lecture and public debate. Our ages ranged from me — the baby of the team at 21 — to Bob Hawkes — well into his 40's.

The team members were: Carl Cash, labor market analyst,

Richmond, VA; George Conn, alumni services field secretary, Northwestern University, Evanston, IL; Chuck Dancke, social security claims adjuster, Danville, IL; Reverend Jack Chase, pastor, Four Squares Church, St. Maries, ID; Wally Frost, teacher, Artesia, CA; Bob Hawkes, graduate student, U of I; Louise Jones and her husband, Tom, sportscaster and writer, WCIA-TV, Champaign; Fritz Krauth, accountant, Long Beach, CA; Dick Maduro, city clerk and treasurer, Madeira Beach, FL; Dean Nosker, assistant editor, College of Agriculture, U of I and his wife and mother of two kids, Lola Lange Nosker; Paul Sones, graduate student, MIT, Boston, MA; Harry Stewart, lawyer, Chicago, IL; Don Swift, placement officer, non-academic personnel, U of I; Frank Vecera, commercial artist, Los Angeles, CA and Donna Weisinger, secretary, IBM Corporation, Oak Park, IL.

We'd become wheelchair users in a variety of ways. Donna, Louise, Jack, Lola, Dean, Wally and I had had polio. Carl, George, Frank, Harry and Dick had become traumatic paraplegics in automobile accidents. Don had been wounded in the attack on Anzio in World War II. Bob had risked his life to rescue a boy in an accident with a tractor at the residential school he headed in Maine. Paul had exited through the canopy of his jet plane when it failed to open as he was in training at the air force academy.

Even Tom Knowles didn't expect 18 people in wheelchairs to tackle Africa without some backup, so eight people not in wheelchairs were chosen to accompany the team. They were: Chuck Elmer and Gibb Fink and Bob "Sergeant Bilko" Wright from the U of I SRC; Paul Luedtke, co-owner of Carter's Mayflower Moving, Urbana, IL; Charlie Ryder, physical education teacher and U. S. National Wheelchair

Sports official, Long Island, NY; Jim Nugent, free-lance writer for Walt Disney Studios, Los Angeles, CA — and Tim's brother — and Roger Ebert, who was warming up as a film critic on the staff of the Champaign-Urbana News Gazette; Dr. Echo Dell Pepper — who'd always wanted to see Africa — and Chuck Dancke's wife, Adrienne, who had been one of my roommates in college — were added to the roster to help close the gender gap. We all wanted Henry Bowman to be part of the team, but South Africa would admit no blacks.

At the last minute, Lola's father died and she chose to remain at home and support her mother.

The group was scheduled to leave in June right after the close of the National Wheelchair Games in New York. May was an unsettling month. Although Tom Knowles had pushed over 200 miles from Grahamstown to Durban to raise funds, he hadn't raised enough. We thought the trip was off. Tim borrowed funds. The trip was on. No airline could be found to carry 17 people in wheelchairs from New York to Johannesburg. We thought the trip was off. Alitalia Airlines welcomed us. The trip was on. What about visas? The trip was off until the South African consulate in Chicago convinced the U.S. consulate to put the trip back on.

With our passports and visas in hand, we were starting to feel confident. Actually, we were naive. The U.S. Department of Health let us know that they didn't care if we left the country, but they weren't going to let us back in unless we'd had inoculations for not only the usual diseases required of overseas travelers, but — because we'd be in Africa — vaccinations for yellow fever, encephalitis and cholera. None of the medical facilities in Champaign-Urbana — or even Chicago — had access to those vaccines. Cancel the trip again! Once again, the United States Air Force came to the rescue. They flew the needed vaccines into Chanute and, by bending the rules a bit, inoculated all of us. We loved the looks on the faces of air force recruits waiting to go into the vaccination clinic when they saw 18 people in wheelchairs coming out. Had their recruiting officer told them everything about the air force?

Paul Luedtke, trained by years in the moving industry, "cubed the area" of our most likely transport in Africa and set the rules for what we could take on the trip — one suitcase apiece — weighing no more than 35 pounds. After all, we had to carry our wheelchairs and athletic equipment, not to mention enough parts and tools to make sure the wheeled equipment would make it through the trip.

Louise and I panicked. Thirty-five pounds in one suitcase was OK for a weekend, but six weeks? It's winter in South Africa. What is winter in South Africa? What do they wear in South Africa? Could we buy makeup there? Had tampons reached South Africa — or did women still use leaves?

"One suitcase," Paul repeated, "or you stay home."

How to get to New York was solved by including all of us on the U of I Gizz Kid team to the National Games. We'd pick up Carl, Frank, Fritz and the others in New York, where they would compete for their own teams. The NWAA invited us to compete for the U.S. when we returned from Africa via England. In those days, 17 free bodies who could compete for the red, white and blue were a bonus that thrilled the National Wheelchair Athletic Association.

Competing in the National Games in that era was full of challenges beyond how fast you could swim or how many arrows you could put in the bull's-eye. You wore your uniform at all times because you knew the transportation to the sports venue would get you there just in time to avoid being disqualified as a no-show. Wheelchair sports have evolved into specialties. Marathon runners today usually don't do field, for example. Back then, everybody was a potential pentathalete. Athletes today miss the thrill of shooting archery for three hours in 50-degree weather with your wet swimsuit slowly soaking through your sweat suit.

As the Illinois coaches and managers packed the bus with equipment and a lot of medals to head back to Illinois with most of the team, the 26 headed for Africa prepared for the unknown. Several of the guys who were veterans used their status to raid the supply rooms at Brooklyn Naval Base. Others of us were assigned to find some place to wash team laundry. Charlie Ryder's wife and neighbors fed us a last meal in the backyard of Charlie's Long Island home.

Alitalia left JFK airport late that night. No one had correctly estimated how long it would take to load 17 gimps, 20 some wheelchairs, equipment for track, field, basketball, archery and maintenance and a few hundred pounds of unidentified necessities.

Sleeping on a plane — even in the days before airlines decided to cram 25% more seats into the cabins — was not a restful experience. We were eager to get out of the confining seats and move around when the plane landed at London's Heathrow.

"Everybody has to stay on the plane," Paul Leudtke told us. "The British ministry of health will not allow people in wheelchairs to enter the country without the proper procedures and transportation to the terminal arranged and supervised by Sister Mercy."

"That's ridiculous," Chuck said. "All we were going to do was stretch, use the bathrooms and rest while the plane is refueled. Our visas have England on them."

"Sorry," Paul said. "That entry is for when we come back for the Games only. All I'm being told is those are the rules."

Alitalia personnel brought food aboard and helped our seven able-bodied men carry us to the plane's bathrooms. Louise, Donna and I realized that modesty would be something we could re-learn when we finished this trip. You better be good friends with any guy who has to stuff you into the lavoratory on a Boeing 707. Refueling and other chores completed, Alitalia took off for Rome.

We hadn't been in the air long when one of the Alitalia officers took Chuck aside.

"Alitalia apologizes for not being able to bend British rules. But, they're arranging for us to stop over in Rome so we can rest and bathe — which, I'm noticing, would improve being around you guys."

Alitalia spared no expenses. A bus met us at Leonardo da Vinci Airport. The Italian driver wasn't going to have anyone think that Romans aren't the most hospitable people in the world, so he took an impromptu tour of the city on the way to the hotel. The lobby of that hotel, with seemingly acres of marble floors, inlaid woods, statues and trees, made even our irrepressible bunch speechless.

Not for long, though. When we got up to our rooms, we were too excited to lie down and sleep. Our first taste of Old World culture needed to be fully explored. Nobody closed the doors to their rooms and bits and pieces of conversation floating up and down the hall was a play by play of discoveries.

"Hey! My bathroom's got two toilets and their both accessible! One's kind of big..."

"That's a bidet, you jerk! Don't you ever read anything?"

"OK. Who hung their underwear out on the balcony to dry? There's a bellman who says a couple of kids in the lobby want to sell the crazy Yanks some underwear — it's already got your name tags sewn in it..."

Maybe we slept. We sure ate, soaked in big marble tubs and ate some more. Alitalia wanted to make sure we knew what the hotel chefs could do.

The driver who took us back to the airport didn't want to be outdone by the first one, so we had another tour of the Coliseum, the Vatican and other sights. After all, it was our plane and they wouldn't leave until we got there.

It was a long flight to Johannesburg. Africa is one long continent and, of course, South Africa is at the bottom. By this time, the Alitalia crew had become part of the team so they accepted the criticism our ex-airmen, Fritz, Paul Sones, Bob Wright and George offered — like Boeing should do some redesign to keep the emergency exits from popping open when we landed in Athens. We stayed on the plane in Athens and during the short refueling stop in Narobi.

When we deplaned at Johannnesburg's Jan Smuts airport, we'd been on a plane for approximately 30 hours over the past two days. The rings around our eyes made us look like a pack of pandas.

chapter 11

Brits, Afrikaaners and Bantus

One way Tom Knowles had managed to fund the trip was by having service groups — like the Lions and Rotary — around South Africa volunteer to have team members stay in their homes during the tour. It was a strange feeling to say good night to the rest of the team, get into a car with people you'd just met and drive off to an unknown destination in a new country. My apprehension was heightened more than a little when we reached the home of my host. He opened the electric gate in the high fence that surrounded his house and called out to two of the largest dogs I'd ever seen. "African lion dogs." he explained. "Part mastiff, part ridgeback — mean buggers. Eat any Kaffir that comes about, you know."

My host offered me a pistol as he showed me to my bedroom. I declined. It wasn't that I didn't know how to shoot nor did I have any qualms about protecting myself. It was just that, whatever got over that fence, remained uneaten by the dogs and tore the iron bars off my bedroom window would be super-human and immune to bullets. I was too tired to figure out that night that houses in South Africa have no central heating. The residents couldn't have windows that opened for security reasons, so houses had holes in the walls near the ceiling for ventilation. Night temperatures in Johannesburg in mid-winter only drop to about 30 degrees. Thirty degrees feels damned cold when you wake up in the morning. Fortunately, the servant brought hot tea just before dawn and an "electric fire."

My host and hostess were delightful. Breakfast was spent comparing our cultures. Naomi found it hard to understand that, back in the states, I cooked my own meals, did my laundry and cleaned my house. She thought her solution to homemaking much more sensible. For approximately $14 a month, she was able to hire a house maid/cook and her gardener/handyman husband. Unlike some of her friends, Naomi was unable to get permission from the government to have her black couple live in, so they left before sundown and walked back to their shack in the township compound outside Johannesburg. Naomi's couple was more fortunate than some in that they had been able to get papers and work permits which allowed them to live together.

We'd all read the book "The Ugly American." Not wanting to be some of those, we'd taken cram courses in the history and lifestyle of South Africa before leaving. We knew that South Africa, like the United States, had been inhabited by natives before Europeans emigrated to the country. Much as the early Americans had slaughtered the Indians, the Dutch and British had slaughtered Zulus, Xhoses, Bantus and other native Africans as the Europeans claimed the land.

But, there were far more native Africans than native

Americans. Although South Africa had begun the practice of separate nations — similar to the Indian reservations in the U.S. — blacks still out-numbered whites in South Africa by more than five to one.

To control the blacks, the South Africans had developed the system of apartheid, which relegated each citizen to one of seven classifications. For a member of the lower classifications, which included the Bantus and colored, to try to cross the lines was fatal. All citizens must carry their government papers at all times and travel was tightly controlled. By limiting educational and employment opportunities and other means of suppression, the whites had been able to keep the blacks controlled. In fact, they had managed to maintain the blacks in a primitive, child-like status. The old missionary pledge "to care for our little dark-skinned brothers" had been raised to new — and malignant — levels in South Africa.

Our first day in Johannesburg established the schedule for the rest of our tour. We would give a demonstration of athletic events in the morning, be the guests of a civic or business group at lunch, give another exhibition in the afternoon, attend a cocktail party in our honor, then, usually, a dinner hosted by yet another group.

As the sun began to rise that first morning, a car arrived at the house and I was picked up to rejoin my teammates at our first appearance for the day at the Randfontein Estates Mines. The visit began with a tea at which mine officials greeted us. We were told that any of us that could pick up a kilo bar of gold could keep it. The sides of the bar sloped and we discovered that pure gold has an oily, slippery surface.

We were then escorted to the upper stopes — or working areas — of the mines. Carts of gold were brought to the surface from lower levels, where men were removing it from the veins in the earth. We were shown the stringent checking systems used to keep men from stealing gold. As we were given the tour, we learned that the lives of the black miners were very restricted ones. They lived apart from their families in camps controlled by the mine companies, ate the food given them and worked the long hours required. On Sunday, their day off, the mine owners encouraged them to work off any energy they had left by participating in tribal dancing. They dressed in the tribal costumes and competed with men from other tribes for small treats from the mine owners. One mine official assured us that the pleasure the men got from these Sunday competitions was just one of the indications that the natives were very child-like in nature and needed the care of the white owners.

If you bought that line of reasoning, you found it logical that another way the white man helped these "little dark-skinned brothers" was by introducing them to civilization. Mine workers were recruited from native villages. Young men were encouraged by their village chiefs to work in the mines — if we understood the convoluted explanation given by the mine owners correctly — because some of their pay went back to the village. The chief then had the funds to pay various taxes levied on his village by the government.

The position of the black native in the South African social structure was made more evident to us when we were taken to visit the school where newly-recruited miners, fresh from the villages, were trained for their jobs. The white tour guide explained that the "boys" were culturally hundreds of years behind the Europeans. In the first training area, for example, he pointed out, the "boys" were being trained to use a shovel, a task so unknown to them that the mine officials made sure they wore covering on the backs of their hands to prevent scraping their skin off against rough rock walls. They also had to be taught to wear boots and learn to recognize and avoid the blisters that could result on their feet. The native, the guide explained, really is unaware of how to avoid injury and has a high tolerance for pain.

Our next guide showed us how the mine owners provided an opportunity to native "boys" to advance. Some of them, he noted, had intelligence and could learn to be boss boys, who, with proper white supervision, could lead crews of other "boys." Since the natives couldn't read or write — or even speak a common language — the mine owners had developed primitive tests to sort out boys with intelligence from those — in the mine owners' opinion, at least — without intelligence. The test was simple. A group of boys were presented with the problem of getting a 50-gallon drum filled with water over a seven-foot high wooden barrier. The boy who figured out how to organize the others to use a rope sling to pull the barrel up on one side of the barrier and lower it down the other side became a boss boy and advanced to boss boy school.

At boss boy school, the native was given the opportunity to learn operation of mechanical equipment and to read and write Funakalo, a language created by the whites in South Africa using words from English, Afrikaans, Portuguese and some Bantu dialects. We heard varying stories about the origin of the language. Some said it was created so that black natives could learn a common language quickly. Others said it was to keep the blacks from becoming too proficient in English or Afrikaans, and therefore, being able to eavesdrop on conversations in households where they were servants. Considering that many of the natives were able to master mechanical equipment, learn Funakalo and memorize a 120-page manual on mine procedures in about six weeks, we suspected that our hosts' concerns about being able to keep the blacks suppressed for much longer was realistic.

The visit to the mines was an immediate immersion in a very different culture, society and mind-set for us. We tried to compare the blacks we had seen with our black friends in the United States. Impossible. Frank, our official team cynic, remarked to me that it wasn't that hard to understand how paternalism could turn malignant with the protector using protection as an excuse for oppression. After all, he added, wasn't that the way most rehab people treated crips?

Our first demonstration of sports that afternoon at the Wanderers Club athletic field was well received. When the guys decided to play football as an encore, we discovered that a rugby ball is a poor substitute for a football. The round ends made the ball almost impossible to pass. The matter was corrected two days later when an incoming Lufthansa airline crew surprised us with a real American football that they'd picked up for us in New York. My sweet little double-recurve, 25-pound pull fiberglass archery bow had been left behind in New York. Dick Maduro loaned me his spare 40-pound pull steel bow. For the rest of the trip, it was a toss-up whether I was going to shoot the arrow or the bow was going to fling me in the other direction.

Our teams had always played basketball on hardwood and football on packed dirt. We immediately learned to play on a combination of grass and loose dirt. Because Lola had been forced to cancel the trip, we were short one girl for the square dancing routines. After a discussion among the male team members, Bob Hawkes "volunteered" to fill in. Gibb and Tom Knowles came up with a platinum blond wig and some pretty astounding falsies; Adrienne did a quick make-up job and our sex symbol, Roberta, emerged. He had an advantage over Donna, Louise and I in that he was strong enough to leap the ruts in the field as we did allemande left and do si do.

As we finished the exhibition, we learned that the people hosting Paul Luedtke and Paul Sones probably weren't the average South Africans. Their first night, Luedtke and Sones had been treated to a meeting of blacks and whites — and it sounded a little like the object was to organize subversive activities. Fortunately, the two Pauls were the coolest heads in the group and, we hoped, would be able to not become involved in the activities. As far as we knew, there was no writ of habeas corpus in South Africa. If you went to jail, they forgot where they put you.

Tom Knowles was still trying to raise the money needed to complete the tour. At one event in Johannesburg, he had Wally Frost play the part of "American Auctioneer" and sell tickets to an upcoming professional sporting event. Knowles also arranged wagers on races between himself and some of our men. Figuring he had about tapped out the resources of Johannesburg, Knowles changed the schedule and roused us out for a quick trip to Pretoria for more fund raising.

Between the receptions, sports demonstrations and teas, we gaped at luxurious sub-tropical flora. Even in the middle of winter, Poinsettias as high as houses, Bougainvilla and plants we didn't recognize bloomed in the parks and around the government buildings. From our hosts, we learned that a good number of the members of government had also been members of the Nazi Party, who were welcomed in South Africa after the defeat of the Third Reich. We thought this was yet another contradiction in the intricate structure of South African society. Jews ranked in the upper categories of the racial definition system which placed blacks, coloreds and Indians at the low end of the class structure. Yet, the Jews seemed to tolerate the former — and probably, philosophically, still — Nazi's.

We returned to Johannesburg with at least enough money to keep the tour going and used Jo'burg as our base for trips to exhibitions in nearby cities. One of the exhibitions we remembered most clearly was at Baragwaneth Hospital for natives, outside Johannesburg, where we learned another lesson in the brutality of life in South Africa. Baragwaneth had a huge patient population of natives with spinal cord injuries which, a doctor explained, were deliberately inflicted by the natives who controlled the social order in the mine compounds. Men from different tribes retained old tribal hostilities and some of the natives preyed on the others. When the men were paid the portion of their wages they got to keep, gangs of outlaws, calling themselves "totsies," routinely stole the money. To maintain a level of fear, the "totsies" didn't kill the other miners. Knowing that death was preferable to disability, the gangs would sever the spinal cords of one or two men with sharpened bicycle spokes as a warning to others. Since the injured natives' fellow villagers would kill them if they returned crippled, they were left with living the rest of their lives at Baragwaneth.

The hospital officials applauded as our men played basketball on a field so rough that they had to back around the court because the casters of their chairs couldn't overcome the ruts. Dick, Bob Hawkes and I were quickly stopped when we brought out our archery equipment. The doctors figured it wasn't a good idea to tempt the patients with sharp weapons.

Our first week flew by with daily trips to the surrounding towns. We soon discovered that we were celebrities — something new after being considered a freak show in the states. Children swarmed around us begging for autographs — and the coins in our pockets. Businessmen from General Motors, Standard Oil, Pepsi and other U.S. firms entertained us, eager for news from home. The press in South Africa was tightly controlled. Television was not allowed. The businessmen assumed correctly that news from the states was frequently distorted or censored altogether. Personnel at the U.S. consulates that entertained us, complained that being posted to South Africa wasn't fun. You couldn't go out after dark and the news of uprisings in the Congo, not too far to the north, was unsettling.

A new activity was added to our schedule. Doctors who saw our exhibitions pleaded for us to split up and visit their hospitals. We must have covered every children's hospital in the country. The native children with bone tuberculosis and rickets, we were told, were indications that health care for natives was still very poor.

We even picked up camp followers. One man followed us around with bottles of water from Lourdes, intent on curing us all of our disabilities until Bob Wright lost his temper and chased him off with logic only Wright could have come up with — "If you cure them, what will I have for a wheelchair team, you idiot?"

Our itinerary was working us southward until, when we reached the edge of the Kalahari Desert, we would fly to Cape Town. As we approached Grahamstown, Tom Knowles' home, the transportation gremlin — who obviously was an invisible member of the team — struck again. Our bus blew a tire, then a second. Swearing, our able-bodied men roused themselves from their naps and went to change the tires. They soon returned.

"The jack they're carrying wouldn't lift a Volkswagon," Chuck swore. "It doesn't matter, though. There's only one spare tire."

Paul Luedtke trudged off to find help. A bus sent out from Welkom — the next city we were to visit — actually got into our sight before it belched a puff of smoke and died. Fortunately, the mayor of Welkom was following in his car so he could go back and rouse the citizens of the town to come rescue us with their cars.

My hostesses in Welkom were two Afrikaaner sisters, who farmed nearby. They spoke almost no English and were dressed in jackets and skirts that looked just like the movie depictions of safari hunters — complete with the boots. Since the only word in Afrikaans I'd learned translated into "get out of here and never come back" and my German was limited to "Good morning, please, thank you, Merry Christmas and shithead," our conversation soon lapsed into smiles and gestures.

They did convey the fact that they didn't get many visitors and that they were really going to feed this one to the limit. By bedtime — determined by the end of daylight due to the absence of electricity on the farm — I was stuffed with food and ready for sleep. The bedroom was rustic, but I grew up on a farm. I knew that the pitcher and basin on the wash stand was the bath part of bathroom. The chamber pot that the ladies pointed out under the bed was the other part.

I appreciated the battery torch the ladies had given me when I heard snuffling and shuffling behind the door across the hall. Peeking through the crack, I saw a large brown eye peeking back at me — from a long, fuzzy gray face — followed by the unmistakable rusty pump sound of Eeeah, Eeeah, Eeeah Haw.

It gets cold in winter on the Transvaal. The body heat from the animals who shared the house with us helped us keep warm. The bed was a little high, but I managed to climb up on it, then plunged way down — into the first feather bed I'd ever met. No alarm clock was needed. My long-eared friend across the hall told us he was hungry just before sunrise.

The sisters seemed to find nothing unusual about having to haul their guest out of the depths of the feather bed when my efforts to climb the sides failed. They'd prepared a little six-course breakfast for me before taking me into town to rejoin the team.

We finished our tour of the Transvaal and parts of the Orange free state, demonstrating sports, lecturing and eating. We loved the small towns. Zululand took us back in time a couple of centuries. The Reverend Jack Chase insisted Paul Leudtke shoot a series of photos with Jack, balanced on the back wheels of his chair, dancing with a Zulu chieftain and his four bare-breasted wives. Maybe he thought it would give his parishioners back home a different idea of their preacher.

We flew into Cape Town in mid-June, feeling like we'd been gone from the U.S. more than just a couple of weeks, but very aware that we hadn't had a day off since we landed in Johannesburg. If you're going to have a day off, there can't be a better place in the world to have it than in Cape Town. The area, settled by the Dutch in the mid-1600's, had nearly 250 years of history before the idea of Johannesburg was even conceived. The climate, similar to the northern Mediterranean Coast, made it ideal for vineyards and farms. The people who settled in Cape Town had lived through the challenges of multiple races and cultures and, even though colored, had relatively few rights and privileges, Cape Town had little of the racial tension and armed camp atmosphere of the northern areas of South Africa.

Again, we were treated like visiting royalty. Donna and I had a whole wing of a house owned by a Cape Town physician — and our own servants. We hit a new high in celebrity status when our pictures appeared in all the papers as we paraded through the center of the city. Actually, being somewhat tired from the morning sports demonstration, we made it up the hill by grabbing on to the nearest car carrying dignitaries and letting them pull our chairs. Not excellent in terms of safe wheelchair use, but it did give us a free hand to wave to the people on the sidewalks.

Rested up from our day off — which, of course, Donna, Adrienne, Louise and I spent shopping — we started in again with our schedule of three appearances per day. The perpetual birthday party started by accident when Donna's and my host and hostess discovered that it was my birthday. Not only that, but Donna's had been the week before and

Chuck Elmer's, the day before Donna's. The birthday party they threw was so much fun that, as we moved up the southeast coast of South Africa, we let it slip that it was our birthday. The parties gave us something to do after our last evening appearance. We were into mid-July — and Rhodesia — before we stopped celebrating our birthdays.

As we had in Johannesburg, we used Cape Town as a base to visit nearby towns such as Paarl and Stellenbosch. Since we were a pretty non-controversial subject, the South African press had publicized our visit well and we began to see more and more "Sold Out" signs as we arrived for exhibitions. One reporter even added a new act to our routine. When the reporter challenged us, saying that we were not really disabled because we had no blankets on our laps and pushed our chairs too fast, Jack Chase decided that he and Fritz Krauth should balance on their chairs on the back wheels, flip over backward and crawl back into the chair. This convinced the reporter that the men were disabled, but Chase and Krauth decided the females should be equally represented. It was a very good thing that skirts were long and fairly tight in those days. The crowds loved it.

After sold-out appearances — and many meals, each more lavish than the previous as the South Africans equated their civic worth to the amount and quality their cooks could produce — we headed up the southeast coast to places including East London, King Williams Town and Port Elizabeth. Each town crammed in the most events possible to protect their civic reputations. At one point, this resulted in our hosts driving us a total of 76 miles between exhibitions to give us the chance to briefly watch some elephants eating oranges on a small game preserve. Another time, our lunch was served as we balanced precariously on little personnel transport vehicles while touring an auto plant. Frank, Dean and Chuck Dancke bagged a couple of Springbok on an early morning hunting trip before the exhibitions started.

Then, we headed for Durban. Durban, an Indian Ocean seaport, was the winter playground for people from inland cities like Johannesburg. "Durban July" is a festival lasting several weeks, attracting thousands of people wanting to get away from Johannesburg and Pretoria's harsh 40-degree dead of winter. We got a couple of afternoons off this time. Dick Maduro organized a trip to the race track. Some of us had front row positions at a rugby match between the South African Springboks and the British Lions. Captains of deep sea fishing boats invited us as their guests. Paul Luedtke rescued the huge fish, caught by our lads, from those of us who were about to roast them over a bonfire on the beach and rushed them to a taxidermist, who shipped them back to the states.

For many of us, the Indian Ocean was the first ocean in which we ever swam. When the cool night temperatures drove us indoors from our beach frolics, we found Durban had a lively nightlife. Those of us who had led more sheltered lives found out why it's called "strip tease." I really don't totally recall why I was sitting on the lap of a nightclub comedian, measuring his mustache when a newspaper photographer was shooting photos for the next day's edition. I just know the picture is still in my scrapbook.

If it sounds like we ate our way across the continent, we did. We learned not to ask questions about what we were eating the day that several of us complimented our hostess on a dish that seemed to be dried sausage. She offered to give us the recipe which began with, "when you make biltong, you should be sure the donkey is young and tender." My god! We just ate Winnie the Pooh's fuzzy friend Eeyore!

Landing once more at Johannesburg's Jan Smuts airport was a homecoming. Our host families from our first days in South Africa grabbed us and whisked us home, keeping us up half the night to listen to our adventures. They crammed our remaining days and nights with so many appearances that we frequently worked in pairs or groups of three. I'm not sure what ground the others covered, but I remember getting the string of my archery bow caught in my earring — the pain of which caused me to accidentally release the arrow prematurely. A panicked zoo employee stopped the photo session, claiming that I'd nearly impaled their lion with my arrow. To demonstrate my remorse, I posed for the next shots with one of their boa constrictors draped across my lap.

Goodbyes at Jan Smuts were tearful. We didn't know if we'd ever see the people we'd grown so fond of again. We didn't know if we'd ever learn the ending to such stories as those of our friends' families under house arrest. We were pretty sure that our letters back when we arrived home in the states might well be censored when they entered South Africa.

chapter 12

The smoke that thunders — and man-eating hippopotami

The next part of our tour was a little more risky than South Africa. While we sometimes nearly became involved in some of the racial problems in South Africa — like the time two of our men found out the house where they were staying was also a meeting place for dissidents advocating overthrow of the white regime by blacks — we were now headed for the Rhodesias. A few years after our visit, Northern Rhodesia would become Zimbabwe. Southern Rhodesia would become Zaire and Nyasaland, Maui. But, as we headed toward the equator, those countries were only entering the process of change from white to black rule. Unlike South Africa, these three smaller countries did not leave the British protectorate to avoid the change of government. Britain would strive to bring about peaceful transition, perhaps having learned a lesson from the experience of the Belgians, who saw blood running in the streets in Elizabethville and Stanleyville as thousands of Europeans were slaughtered during the transition of government.

It turned out that we were only in some potential danger when we appeared in Kitwe, a copper-mining town across the border from Elizabethville. That trip was ill-conceived for a number of reasons.

Our hosts, the governments of northern and southern Rhodesia, had assigned us our very own plane from the Royal Rhodesian airline fleet. That DC-3 must have been the first airplane old man Douglas ever built. McDonnell probably hadn't even been born. And to go with our very own plane, we had our very own crew. Our Captain, Ted Krueger, was an instant hit with our former air force men — especially Bob Wright. Ted told us he was an ex-RAF pilot who'd had a few "dust-ups" with the Jerrys in WWII, flown for BOAC until he left part of his Boeing 707 behind on a sticky take-off from Rome, then moved on to Royal Rhodesian. Our acceptance of his tales was tempered a little by the fact that he also drank Scotch for breakfast — and lunch — and dinner — and tea. But Ted proved to be one hell of a good pilot.

The fact that Luedtke, Wright and Ted spent a lot of time in conference before the trip should have given us a clue that this was going to be a bit different. Then we found out about the restrictions Kitwe air field held even for our tiny DC-3.

"Tomorrow for the trip to Kitwe," Paul announced, "you'll be allowed 10 pounds of luggage. Leave the rest of your stuff here and we'll pick it up when we get back. You three heavier guys can look out for it because we can't take you either. Seems the runway's a bit short and Ted has to have minimum weight to take off for the flight back."

That there was an airstrip at Kitwe seemed doubtful. Fritz lost his composure and asked Ted if he planned to land in the river — or the trees — as we began the descent. Ted waved over his shoulder and took us through a parting in the trees and pulled the plane to a stop on the river bank.

Our sports demonstrations were well received in Kitwe. And we toured a copper mine this time. Some person, who said they were from the International Red Cross, got a little uptight about 17 people in wheelchairs being across the river from Moishe Tschombe, who wasn't particularly known for his humanitarian traits. If it had ever occurred to his forces — like it occurred to the Red Cross person — to take us hostage, they probably would have found us too much trouble to keep.

The Royal Rhodesian DC-3 stole our attention from demonstrations and lectures though. We were flying along one day when I poked George — who after all had been in the air force and knew about planes — and asked if that black stuff running across the wing really was oil. He assured me that Ted could probably make it to our destination even with that engine turned off. Ted did. On the next trip, we were flying along when a loud noise, a sudden draft and the sound of wind rushing by alerted us to the fact that the cabin door had flown open. Responding to Ted's request, "Will you blokes close the bloody door?" Chuck, Gibb, Bob Wright and Paul Luedtke and Roger Ebert formed a human chain, holding one another around the waist until Bob could be dangled forth to reach the flapping door and close it.

When the door stayed closed and the engine didn't spurt

oil, Ted delighted in what seemed suspiciously like stunt flying. He gave us tree top tours so we could get a good look at the Sable antelope, a sight seen by few tourists — including those of us who closed our eyes. Ted herding elephants with the plane resulted in one of the guys, ignoring George's best attempts at anti-airsickness counseling, tossing his cookies in a team duffel bag. But probably the act we liked best was when Ted would buzz runways to scare off the baboons. You have to get pretty close to scare a baboon.

The Rhodesias, being closer to the equator, differed in temperature and landscape. The Rhodesias differed from South Africa in political climate, as well. Here, natives attended our exhibitions and talked freely with us. They held clerical jobs and wore the uniform of the army of Northern Rhodesia. They were eager for the British to turn over the country to their new government.

The Rhodesias, unlike South Africa, had sent teams to the International Wheelchair Games in Stoke-Mandeville, England. Our competition in demonstrations was with experienced athletes. Hawkes and Maduro held their own against excellent Rhodesian archers. I hit the target most of the time, but suspected the Rhodesian women archers held back to make me look less clumsy. George claimed there wasn't a swimming pool in either country with water temperature over 50 degrees.

Most of us stayed in the homes of Rhodesian farmers, a hearty lot, indeed. Faced by unknown changes when the native ruler took over, the Rhodesian farmers had elevated the practice of "Sundowning," which we quickly adopted. The Rhodesians saw the sundown with large quantities of scotch, gin or any other quality alcohol. The fact that there is almost no twilight time that close to the equator mandated that the spirits be consumed quickly lest you be left to face the darkness sober.

We found that the same reckless attitude existed in driving. Only the most daring would drive on what passed for roads in this country. Any two relatively smooth dirt paths, spaced the same width apart as the wheels of a Landrover qualified as a highway. To drive on these roads, the Rhodesian centered his vehicle squarely on the two tracks and took off at top speed. Vehicles coming from the opposite direction did likewise. When two vehicles were heading at breakneck speed toward one another, some signal or rule — which none of us ever discovered — caused one to swerve off the road before head-on collision.

If you didn't kill yourself on the road, the animals might do you in if your home was Rhodesia. More than once, we were greeted by our hosts with accounts of a native being killed by a hippopotamus, a prize bull being carried off by a leopard or a villager being attacked by a lion. The conversation among the farmers gathered at my host's house one evening focused on such a lion, who being too old or too injured to hunt normal prey, had begun to rely on the farmers' barnyards for food. I'd just fallen to sleep in the rather remote wing of the house when a sound — to my thinking, very much like a large animal sniffing — awoke me. A paw reached in the partially open window, pulling it all the way open. A large, furry head appeared, followed by a body. Not screaming was no carefully considered act on my part. To scream, you have to be breathing. When I started breathing, the light from the farmyard through the window showed that my "lion" was actually the family German Shepherd, who was somewhat perturbed to find his family had loaned out his bed for the night.

Life for people with disabilities in Rhodesia also differed from that of their counterparts in South Africa. One of my hostesses, Diane — whose last name I lost years ago — owned her farm and supervised the running of it. We found that we had had polio in the same year and at the same age. Diane, like me, had chosen to carry on, viewing her wheelchair as part of the bargain. For me, it was like being back in the dormitory at U of I — no sleep as the two of us talked through the night comparing experiences.

After over a month since our arrival in Johannesburg, we gave our last exhibition in Fort Victoria. The hugs and tears we shared with the people who had been our hosts and hostesses signalled another parting from people we weren't sure we'd ever see or hear from again.

But, our treat from the Rhodesian government was a "holiday" — nearly a week at Victoria Falls and Wanke Game Preserve in Northern Rhodesia. We were finally going to get to be tourists. Better yet, Ted Krueger, our co-pilot, Erik and our intrepid DC-3 were going with us.

Ted woke us up from our dozing by taking the plane into the mist of Victoria Falls — which the natives named, "The Smoke that Thunders." It wasn't until Dr. Livingston got lost — and found by his rescuer, Mr. Stanley — that the Falls were discovered by white men. They promptly claimed them for Britain and named them after their Queen Victoria.

"It looks like a set for a John Wayne movie," Donna said as we were driven up to Victoria Falls Hotel. A wide veranda faced the falls so that we could "sundown" while watching the mists catch the last of the sunlight.

"I could sacrifice and become a Colonist real quick, if this came with it," Donna remarked. "I wouldn't even care if the rest of the world criticized me." We settled into our room — approximately the size of both of our apartments put together back in the states — and Donna pulled on a fancy tapestry rope on the wall. She grinned in satisfaction when a servant appeared immediately, greeted us and left to return with Pepsi's and snacks. "Think they'll let me take one home to help out?" she asked.

Our first day we wandered along paths that went through the jungle to the very edge of the falls. We bartered with natives for the animal and human figures they were carving out of wood, commenting on their sense of enterprise. We found out how enterprising they were when we discovered that they were sneaking into the jungle to sell their crafts to avoid splitting the profits with the government sponsored "native craft village" we visited later that day. That night, we reasoned that we could sleep in England — or when we got back to the states — and stayed up to watch the rare lunar rainbow created by Victoria Falls.

To visit Wanke, the group would have to split into two groups. There wasn't enough space in the Landrovers or the Rondovel huts in which we were to stay at Wanke to accommodate all of us. Those of us left behind when the first team left for Wanke amused ourselves by taking a trip up the Zambeze River.

"Don't do that!" one of our guides shouted as he pulled at a team member who was trailing his hand in the water. "See those?" "Those," which we had assumed to logs, opened their little yellow eyes and became crocodiles, swimming after the boat.

"I believe it must be time for tea," Dr. Pepper noted as she watched one of the native guides dip a tea kettle over the side of the boat and fill it with water. Louise and I immediately lost our taste for tea, but Dr. Pepper assured us it would be properly boiled and, therefore, safe to drink.

Dr. Pepper took to the jungle with relish. The pictures of her swinging on a vine, imitating Tarzan, were a little underexposed. So were the pictures of the monkey, who climbed into an empty wheelchair and imitated a member of the team.

When half of the team, who considered themselves now qualified as Great White Hunters, returned from Wanke, we refused to listen to their tales of hair-raising adventures. We were too busy getting into the vehicles to go have our own hair raised.

The rangers and guides at Wanke Park weren't about to give us the chance to raise our hair too high. The animals in the park were free and the people kept in cages — or more accurately, vehicles and compounds. The guides told us that nearly every year, they lost some tourist who failed to believe that a bull elephant is more than a match for a car if he chooses to turn it over or sit on it. Tourists also, according to our guides, tended to confuse lions with big pussy cats.

The Rondovels — round houses constructed from mud — were tiny. Meals were served under a thatched roof in the middle of the compound. The generator that provided some electricity was turned off at 9:00 p.m., so we settled around the fire to entertain ourselves.

"Where's George?" someone asked.

"Last time I saw him, he was by the fence, listening to some natives play music — hear that rasping sound?"

"There ain't no natives out there!" Paul exclaimed. "That sound is a lion — more likely a lioness looking for dinner."

Charlie Ryder wandered off to investigate, returning shortly. "He's asleep in his chair."

"Aren't you going to bring him back?"

"Nah. He's far enough inside the fence that the lion couldn't reach him. Besides, I've had to wake George up. He'll hold his own with any lion."

Jannes, the guide who drove the car in which Louise and Tom Jones, Harry Stewart and I rode, was suitably daring. He got in close enough to clearly see the whiskers on a lady lion, doing the family food shopping by killing a water buck. Jannes pulled the Landrover back on the road when she decided we were as pesky as hyenas. Louise and I were less than enthused as we inched through a herd of elephants. Visions of the elephant version of trash compactor, using our vehicle as trash, occurred to us. We shared pretty much the same feeling about the cape buffalo. We were pretty calm about the giraffes, elands, springboks, Thompson gazelles and kudus. We even tolerated chasing wart hogs, figuring they weren't big enough to turn the car over and pry us out. Tom concentrated on shooting miles of film for WCIA-TV. Harry looked forward to meeting his wife in London.

Forty days after we had left New York, we boarded South African airlines at Salisbury airport to fly to London. In that time, seventeen people considered as cripples and eight people considered as able-bodied had covered over 30,000 miles, visited 33 cities, given over 40 demonstrations of sports, lost count of the number of lectures and personal appearances and consumed several tons of food. We'd balanced our chairs on the back wheels to get around the lost ruins of Zimbabwe, prowled through the back streets of Cape Town and Durban and made many friends, some of whom who would come to the states to visit us over the next 30 years. We left behind larger-than-life photos of us in rehab centers and young people with disabilities, who would become our competitors in future international sports meets.

The logistics were overwhelming — if we'd thought about them before carrying them out. Seven men carried the 14 of us, who could not walk at all, off of planes and buses, a tribute to their physical condition. Of course, Roger Ebert weighed about 110 pounds at the time even though he held his own at the feasts provided for us. Paul Luedtke had swiped a trick from the moving trade and numbered each piece of luggage and equipment. Knowing our numbers, we were expected to dump our belongings in the proper order in front of any means of transport we were using that day. If a number was missing, Paul knew the culprit. "We don't move 'til all the numbers are in line." We never lost a piece of our belongings, which included six spare wheelchairs, 25 suitcases, six bags of sports equipment, a portable display, four archery sets, three complete sets of uniforms for the team and a set of portable stairs for Jack Chase to use to demonstrate how to go up and down steps on the rear wheels of the chair.

Probably more remarkable was that we were all speaking to one another when we arrived at Salisbury. Having lived for 40 days in proximity closer than a refugee family of 25 in Hong Kong, we'd naturally had a few spats. But the pressure of our schedule didn't allow much time for arguments. Other than a few upset stomachs and minor sprains, no one had sustained any injuries. We sure knew each other's habits, likes and dislikes after living together. How, we asked, could Chuck Elmer possibly drink luke warm Pepsi when he first got up in the morning?

"As the sun sets over the Rhodesian hills, we board our South African Airways Boeing 707 and bid farewell to our many friends..." Tom Jones' recording session for his TV documentary was cut short by the rest of us throwing whatever was handy to shut him up so we could go to sleep.

chapter 13

"Welcome to international competition ...

W hich strengthens the mind and the spirit as the body grows more able." The speaker was a rosy-cheeked man, a bit rounded in the middle, who looked as though he might have been the inspiration for pictures of St. Nicholas. He was Sir Ludwig Guttmann, a skilled neurosurgeon who had left his native Germany when it became apparent that even neurosurgeons would not escape Hitler's persecution of the Jews. He was instrumental in founding a spinal cord injury treatment center at Stoke-Mandeville, England. His work proved that humans could not only survive spinal cord injury — a premise disputed by most medical authorities in the mid-1940's — but that they could be restored to active lives, even though they'd use wheelchairs for the rest of their lives. Because his methods were so effective, British subjects from around the world were flown to Stoke-Mandeville for treatment following spinal cord injury.

Sir Ludwig believed that the spinal cord injured person was still a whole person. He once left Chicago talk show host, Norman Ross, speechless when Sir Ludwig, George Conn and I were guests on Norman's program. "Now, let's talk about the sex," Sir Ludwig said. In those early days of the 1970's, everyone — except those of us who were disabled — knew that there was no such thing as sexuality after disability. Sir Ludwig may have had first-hand observations of the untruth of that theory. He mingled with the athletes at the International Games at all hours.

Sports of all kinds, Sir Ludwig reasoned, restored self-respect and competitive spirit. In addition, training for those sports was a natural means of strengthening remaining muscles. On this day, he must have been filled with pride at the success of his work in international competition as he stood before the crowd of wheelchair athletes wearing the team colors of 26 nations. "Let the Games begin!" he shouted as the flags of each nation were hoisted on the poles surrounding the basketball "pitch" — outdoor court — that had once been a helicopter landing pad at Stoke-Mandeville.

Our group had arrived in London from Rhodesia earlier in the week. Evidently, the USA team officials were under the impression that, once we got through the red-tape involved in entering England if you were in a wheelchair, we would go directly to Stoke-Mandeville and join the rest of the USA team. We were so worn out from the flight, we didn't even bother fighting being loaded onto special buses and thoroughly scrutinized by Sister Mercy and her cadre of British health official nurses. But, once we hit the front door of Heathrow airport, we scattered. After all, we'd roamed around a lot of Africa independently. We could certainly handle London and the surrounding countryside.

The British citizens on the street immediately recognized us as "Yanks." People in strange-looking wheelchairs, dashing along the streets of London, unaccompanied by nurses or attendants were quite evidently an uncommon sight. Donna, Dean and I enlisted Gibb to be our driver and the four of us pooled our resources to rent an Austin Mini — the biggest car we could afford. We drew comments from passersby when we managed to stack three wheelchairs in the trunk — or boot — in an attempt to visit every corner of London in record time.

Sometimes, it works out better if you aren't aware of customs and traditions. For example, the parking space in the court of St. James Palace seemed like a logical place to leave the Austin so we'd be within short pushing distance of Buckingham Palace. We couldn't go home without pictures of the Changing of the Guard, could we? The Bobby was pretty understanding when we explained that, in the U.S., people put up "No Parking" signs — and they probably should have closed the gate if tourists weren't supposed to be in the courtyard. And, we were really done touring Madame Tussard's Wax Museum when the guard suggested that we leave after Gibb posed as part of one of the exhibits.

We absorbed the sights of London — Piccadilly Circus, Shepherd's Market, Regency Street, Soho, Fleet Street, St. James Park and the Thames. A lot of London looked just as we had imagined when we had read Charles Dickens and studied British history. Despite the inaccessibility of the Tower of London, Tom and Louise Jones toured it all with some arranging done by Paul Luedtke. Jack Chase and Wally Frost found the Tube — London's subway system —

an ideal way to get around town. They had no qualms about guiding their wheelchairs down a flight of steps backward or riding escalators to reach the trains. A rumor grew, as members of the group encountered one another, that Paul Sones had even been invited into Buckingham Palace.

The food had been better in South Africa and the Rhodesias. Dining at a restaurant billed as having American food one night, Fritz Krauth — who was into owning restaurants at that point of his life — pointed out to the management that, in America, it was considered proper to remove the fried potatoes from the grease before serving them — and most of the cooks in America took the stray chicken bones out of the fries as well. Fritz hadn't seen cuisine. He had yet to experience dining at Stoke-Mandeville.

The reception of the athletes returning from Africa by the rest of the USA team was notably chilly. So was the temperature of the "huts" in which we were housed. Unlike the image of a hut which might spring to mind — cozy dwelling for several people with maybe even a fireplace — these huts were huge, barn-like buildings that could house up to 100 people. Men were assigned to huts which two to four nations shared. International competition among women was just beginning, so all 90 women competitors shared the same hut — and four bathrooms. The single beds were too close together to get a wheelchair between them — so you went into the bed over the end. Though the beds were narrow, there was no danger of rolling off. However, through many years of service, the mattresses had developed a permanent depression in the middle, exactly the shape of a human body. If you thought about it too long, you started imagining this was what sleeping in a casket must be like.

Then there was the food. Because Stoke served the entire British Empire, it was spread over many acres. The nurses used bicycles to travel between buildings. Bicycles also towed the food carts to each hut for meals. It was rumored that the kitchens in which the food was prepared were located somewhere in the general vicinity of Stoke-Mandeville, but that was hard to judge from the temperature and condition of the food after it had been towed to the hut in a steam cart.

"What is this?" one of us new arrivals asked a USA Teammate, who had been at Stoke for a week.

"It's roast beef, potatoes, peas and dessert," she replied.

"They boil roast beef in England?"

"It's probably been in the steam cart a while. The hard green things are the peas. The hard grey ones are the potatoes. The soft grey things are gooseberries — they're for dessert."

The quality of food and shelter was forgotten in the excitement of competition and the fun of meeting people from all over the world. Most of us on the USA team felt that the United States had a long way to go in letting people in wheelchairs be part of everyday life, but we soon found that our lives were less confined than those of our foreign counterparts. We did, however, kind of envy the Swedes, for whom the government provided three wheelchairs at a time, all with different purposes — indoor, outdoor and travel. We also envied the German and Italian Teams, whose competition was supported by government funding.

We soon lost some of our confidence that Americans were naturally superior in athletics. Competition was tough. Our fencers were eliminated in the first round by the French and

Germans, many of whom had been professional fencers before injuries during WWII. Those of us who swam frequently found the ferocious Israelis hitting the end of the pool ahead of us. Even our superstars in field, led by Illinois' Tim Harris, who had come close to equalling NCAA distances for discus and javelin, had a major battle to defeat the Argentine superstar in field events. We decided that we would train much harder for next year's competition, but surely, the USA would take the gold for basketball. After all, we'd invented the sport.

It took a while for our men to adapt to the rules for international wheelchair basketball. In addition to the amount of time spent in the key, points for free throws and other fine points of the game, there were other variances. For example, in the U.S., the NWBA required that at least three of the players had to have a disability severe enough to prevent them from carrying their wheelchairs — or their teammates — onto the court. No such eligibility apparently existed in the international rules. The NWBA also recognized such offenses as travelling, double-dribbling and charging as fouls to be rewarded with free throws. Obviously from the way games were played, the only offense in international basketball that warranted a foul call was violent death inflicted by one player on another. Even then, the official had to witness the act of killing — not just the body.

The USA basketball team adapted to play. In fact, they seemed to enjoy committing mayhem without the threat of penalties. In the final round of play, the USA and the Italian team had survived to compete for the gold medal. We all-American kids weren't very fond of the Italian team even before the game. They were allowed to drink even at the training tables. We felt they were poor sports after an Italian swimmer won a race after pulling the swim trunks of a USA swimmer down around his knees in a little cross-lane activity. We were totally up for this last event of the games.

Spectators might have been a bit confused when team members were introduced. The names on the USA team — like Giaccapo, Caputo, Acca, Lapicola and Tardalo — sounded pretty similar to the names of the Italian players. But the origin of their names hadn't created any loyalty to Italy among our squad. When they took the court, they reverted to the early days of wheelchair basketball in the USA — the days when it was considered good defense to sneak up behind a man when he was shooting and tip his chair over backward. They remembered how to come down the court with an opponent's hand being ground between his handrim and yours. And balancing your chair on the back wheels, then slamming your footrests on your opponent's feet — which frequently flung him out of his chair — was a pretty effective defensive move, too.

The war on the court immediately overcame any differences there may have been between the USA and Israeli teams. The Israeli's, two of whom had been sponsored by Pan Am Airways for a year's training in New York, ringed the court. The Italians, being battered on the court, were battered on the sidelines if they ventured out of bounds by Israelis screaming, "Oosaa! Oosaa! Oosaa! Kill! Kill! Kill!" Those Israelis never could remember that USA was pronounced as three letters — not one word. We took the gold home.

chapter 14

In pursuit of gold for the red, white and blue

Over the next four years, I would return to Stoke-Mandeville twice, with the 1965 and 1966 USA teams. I was able to support my desire to compete because of my employment at the SRC while working toward my master of science degree. In addition, the U of I had some of the finest coaches and easily accessed practice areas. Despite my doubts, I really was good in swimming — good enough to gather gold medals in national and international competition and set some records, one of which stood for 12 years.

For many of us, whose lives had been re-directed by physical disability, earning a berth on the USA team was more than just a chance to compete. We certainly beat the role of "shut-in," commonly associated with a disability, as we traveled around the globe. With funding very minimal for the USA team, there was little money available to take many able-bodied trainers and coaches and we usually found ourselves on our own as we explored new lands.

Being on the USA team was a guarantee of adventures in foreign lands. We didn't think we were pretty hot stuff — we knew it. We were well on our way to escaping the stereotype of cripple. Most of us were college graduates. To accomplish that with a disability in the '60's meant that a person had to be aggressive and have above-average intelligence. Constantly running up against preconceived ideas of what people with disabilities were like had turned us to our own brand of cynicism, bordering on arrogance.

Ernest Hemingway was at the height of his popularity and his protagonist, Jake Barnes, in *The Sun Also Rises*, became a role model for us — a physically flawed hell-raiser who tended to over-compensate. It was really quite fortunate that we were based in Madrid while in Spain. If we'd managed to get to Pampalona, surely the macho USA male athletes would have run, using their wheelchairs, with the bulls. Some of them actually discussed the possibility when they spent a rainy afternoon boozing with TV and movie tough guy, Broderick Crawford. We settled for startling the daylights out of Spaniards as we took on the Palace Royale and the Plaza Mayor in droves.

Close quarters at Stoke-Mandeville brought out the best — or worst — of the humor when the West German men's team shared a hut with the USA team one year. The many Jewish lads on our team found it impossible to keep their mouths shut.

"Timmy, Timmy," Richie Rosenbaum yelled one afternoon, as he came into the hut from competition. "Our hut mates are ramping the incinerator — and they just plugged the drains in the showers and put in different shower heads!"

Another time, Richie conducted a demonstration on how to open a can of soda with a foot-long screwdriver, used by the equipment managers to change wheels on the chairs. "Achtung! Make sure you hit only the can. One slip and you become a do-it-yourself Rabbi — or worse, back to the Vienna Boys Choir mit you."

Despite Richie's peculiar brand of diplomacy and the language barriers, the German and USA team members formed close friendships. The Germans had mixed emotions when Saul Welger, USA basketball star, stole the German's star swimmer, Christa, by marrying her and taking her back to New York. Christa anchored the USA's unbeatable women's swim team for several years before retiring to motherhood.

In later years, both U.S. Olympics and U.S. Paralympics would provide decorative pins, representative of the team's nation, for athletes to trade. Back then, we just traded our uniforms. Finally, Ben Lipton and Sy Bloom, the USA team officials who were stuck with raising most of the money to buy the uniforms, finally began charging us a deposit when we were issued our uniforms. Somehow, you thought, as you negotiated for a beautiful sweat suit that said "Suisse" all over it, you'd do without getting the deposit back. Or maybe Willie Wilkins would manage to lose the records of who was supposed to have what.

That we had the opportunity to compete and travel was attributable to the belief — and stubbornness — of relatively few people. Just as there would not have been a National Wheelchair Basketball Association had Tim Nugent not spent what might have been his free time organizing, cajoling the air force into providing transportation and tournament sites and feeding and housing competitors, there would not have been a National Wheelchair Athletic Association if it hadn't been for people like Ben Lipton.

The National Wheelchair Games were held in New York because Ben and his employer, Bulova Watch Company, did the work and carried the costs. Bulova had been one of the first places in the country where men with spinal cord injuries were taught trade skills. While training hundreds of men in skills including watch repair, engraving and other fine-detail work, the Bulova family had become believers in the potential of people with disabilities. Track and field, table tennis and other events were held at the Bulova factory. For nearly a week, the Bulova employees took time from their regular jobs to mark race lanes on the parking lots, chase javelins, discus and shots, prepare meals for several hundred athletes and transport us to other venues, such as the swimming pools of Queens College. Many of them could easily be talked into some side trips for athletes finished with their events.

Tim and Ben had many a heated argument over the best way to give us the best chances to compete. Being lucky enough to work for both men, I was frequently treated to each man's personal philosophy. Tim moved the NWBA Tournaments around the country. Ben rather thought New York was the only place for the Games. Tim insisted the athletes with disabilities run the show — even though he sometimes saw his ideas voted down at meetings. The NWAA administration was closely held and we athletes were usually in the dark. Tim shoved us out on our own. Ben loved to "father" us. Tim's fiery Irish temper and his raging covered endless layers of marshmallow and love. Beneath Ben's gentle, scholarly Jewish mien was steel determination to push us to do our best. Outside of the competition arena, both men had a high respect for each other and the most important thing was that thousands of people with disabilities had the chance to compete in a setting where ability was everything — and the word "disability" banned from all conversations. The NWBA grew even though there was occasional turmoil among the players who led it. The NWAA also has turmoil, which led to it breaking apart for a couple of years and being re-formed as Wheelchair Sports America. Actually, sports associations for athletes with disabilities had pretty much the same fights as the NFL, NHL NBA and the professional baseball associations.

Because I only worked for Ben during the season, and then only in press relations, I never was able to discover how he — and his alter-ego, Seymour Bloom — maneuvered the team's travel opportunities. Ben reasoned that, if he could get his athletes to England, it would be a shame not to get them across the English Channel to Europe. One year, he convinced the French that it would be very valuable to have their team practice against the USA before going to Stoke-Mandeville. All the French had to do was find housing, food and transportation for about a week and Ben would provide stiff competition for final training. And since we were that close to Paris..... He also convinced the Spanish government that it could advance opportunities for its citizens with disabilities by paying for the USA team to visit Madrid.

The French trip had its high points. It was a pleasant surprise for us, upon landing at Orly Airport, that the airline and customs officials had no trouble dealing with over 60 people in wheelchairs deplaning from one jet liner. It grew less pleasant after we boarded the bus which would take us into Paris. While watching us board the bus, the driver said something in French and left. He wasn't back when we were all aboard and our equipment stowed. He wasn't back over an hour later when we finished the soft drinks and snacks our coaches and manager had brought out from the terminal. More time passed and he still didn't return.

"To hell with it," said the same Charlie Ryder who'd managed to survive 30,000 miles of travel to Africa. "I've driven buses at Bulova. How different can it be in French?"

Everybody agreed that we had a vague idea of where we were heading —surely there were road signs and someone had come up with a couple of maps. Many of us were able to even recall a few words of our high school or college French.

"Hey, Charlie!" somebody called out, "I think they drive on the left side of the road here."

"That's in England, you dummy," someone else replied.

"Well, there's a lot of confused Frenchmen out there, then. They all seem to be headed straight at us."

We settled back and admired the increasingly open country side, filled with flowers being grown, we were sure, for la parfum. We commented on the fact that we had really expected Paris to be a big city, not little groups of little houses with lots of fields around them.

"Oh good," someone said. "It's only 29 Km to Avignon."
"What's a Km?" "Where's Avignon?"

But, we were all happy — especially Charlie, who was delighted that his big bus made the little cars scatter as we barreled down the road. Actually, not everyone was happy. The transport company, which owned the bus, was unhappy with its disappearance. The local law officials were not happy about a bus full of people in wheelchairs being driven around France by a person without the equivalent of a French chauffeur's license.

"Hey!" one of the team yelled. "Listen to those crazy French sirens — sounds just like in movies!"

"Look at the cars chasing us with their lights flashing," someone else added.

"You'd better pull over, Charlie," one of the coaches said. "Oh, hell," Charlie replied. "I was just getting the hang of driving a bus on this side of the road."

Men in police uniforms and men in business suits screamed at each other in French for a while. Then a driver came— who had a French driver's license and could even read the signs and maps — and we made our way into Paris. We'd barely begun our exploration of Paris when we were driven on to Fountainbleu.

The only accommodations the French could find for the USA team was a girls' school. The buildings had been ramped so we could enter. So had the two long rows of outdoor toilets that faced each other in the courtyard. The French have always been more relaxed about bodily functions than us uptight descendants of the Puritans. The partial doors on each stall, designed to provide a modesty panel for the middle of a school girl's body, weren't of much help to those of us in wheelchairs. You sort of situated yourself on the splintery wood bench, in appropriate relationship with the hole cut in it — and hunched down behind your wheelchair.

Ben Lipton was always more generous with time off for his teams than Tom Knowles had been in Africa. Sights to see in Fountainbleu were limited. Besides, after years of bickering, the North Atlantic Treaty Organization had reached agreement to pull foreign troops out of France and we weren't able to determine whether the natives of Fountainbleu had developed a dislike for U.S. citizens because of the troops stationed in their town, or whether they were angry at losing the business the troops gave their town. One thing was clear — they were angry at Americans for some reason.

We wisely decided to spend our R & R time at the Royal Chateau in Fountainbleu. The curving staircase, a full story high, would have been an obstacle to about five dozen people using wheelchairs, but the United States Air Force was still stationed near by. Nearly 100 Airmen met us at the Chateau to carry us into and around the interior of the Chateau.

Ben and I were thrilled when one of my photos of the Airmen and the USA team was printed in the news section of The Chicago Tribune, rather than the sports section, where my photos usually ran. Publicity like that would help greatly in the next year's fund raising efforts.

Just as the United States Air Force was a critical factor in launching wheelchair sports through air force support with facilities, personnel and transportation, the sports editors of many papers, particularly in Illinois, had a leading role. It was their stories and friendships that publicized the abilities of people with disabilities. Portrayal of disability in newspapers moved from the human interest — and pity — aspect to the sports page when writers like Dave Condon, of The Chicago Tribune, began to report about skills in terms that sports fans identified. U of I journalism school graduated many excellent sports writers — Rick Talley, Rockford Morning Star, Taylor Bell, Chicago Daily News and Bill White, of the Bloomington, Indiana papers. These men had been friends with wheelchair athletes in college and brought wheelchair sports to their columns. Even better, they hired me as a stringer and photographer when I traveled with the Illinois and USA teams.

Not only did working for the sports editors stave off the starvation always facing a grad student and give me a few extra dollars to spend when travelling, the by-lines were great for the portfolio I was building — hoping to someday go into journalism for real. One time, a downstate paper contacted me to see if I'd like to interview for a sports writer's job. They didn't seem too concerned about the wheelchair bit — but the woman thing bothered them. It would be a lot of years before women would be allowed in locker rooms.

chapter 15

In the land of the
rising sun

The USA wheelchair team didn't spend all of its time on one side of the globe. In 1964, the Paralympics were held in Japan following the Olympics.

The USA planned to include approximately 60 competitors on the team, but they would be chosen from hundreds of athletes, who competed in regional meets then, if they qualified, the National Games in New York. The Illinois Gizz Kids athletes trained as never before. Swimmers arrived at the pool — located illogically in the English Building — to get in two hours of practice before the pool had to be used for physical education classes. We learned a lesson in how the physical plant managed swimming pools. The chlorine level is very high in the morning so it can deteriorate as the day wears on. The water temperature is very cold, so it can warm up as bodies go in and out of it. It evened out for us. The burning of the excess chlorine helped us overcome the freezing temperature of the water. We also learned that it gets cold enough in Illinois to freeze your hair to your head

— especially since the wall-mounted hair dryers in the locker rooms were too high for us to reach from a wheelchair.

The spring was filled with regional competitions. Both our men's and women's swim teams were approaching top shape as the National Games neared. At one meet, Evelyn Mulry pushed beyond her limits and passed out in the pool, which caused Henry Bowman to dive in the pool fully clothed to pull her out. My shoulder was separated when an over-eager swim meet helper grabbed my hand and pulled me out of the pool by one arm before I realized what he was doing. But, like the track and field teams, the swimming team swept all classes at the National Games.

We thought it was pretty neat that Roosevelt Grier, former football star, and Rafer Johnson, Olympic track star, worked at the games as helpers and buddies to the competitors. Somehow, a swimming trophy meant more when it was handed to you by Rosie Grier.

Of course, the NWAA didn't have enough funds to send 60 athletes and their handlers to Tokyo. We were probably happier not knowing how many they could afford to send. The top competitors, who were excellent candidates for multiple gold medals, were informed that their expenses would be entirely paid by the NWAA. But, that didn't excuse even the all-expenses-paid athletes from getting out and raising enough funds to take care of the whole team. A competitor could pay the difference between the allocation from the NWAA and the total cost, but Illinois Gizz Kids didn't have those resources. We literally went out on the street and raffled off a new Corvair, donated by an "Angel" of the U of I SRC — Giles Sullivan. That isn't to say we did it happily as some of us imagined we weren't too different than charity fund raisers. But Tim pointed out that somebody would win the car — then went out and borrowed $8,000 personally to make sure we got there.

A team has to train somewhere, right? In this instance, Ben Lipton decided Hawaii was a good place to train in November. After who-knows-what negotiations, the United States Army of the Pacific agreed that it would be an honor to turn over as much of Fort Derussey as needed for housing, complete with meals, and make any other armed forces facilities on the island available for training.

Most of us expressed the feeling that we were at our peak and further practice would only tire us out for the competition in Toyko. Our coaches, like Junius Kellogg, the Harlem Globetrotter who joined the Pan Am Jets wheelchair basketball team after meeting a tree head on in a car, felt otherwise. The coaches passed out practice schedules that took up all the hours from 8:00 a.m. to 6 p.m. daily. They strongly hinted that we wouldn't want to miss any practices because the boats they'd found to take absentees from practice back to the States weren't all that accessible.

So, we gaped at the scars left on the palm trees around Scofield Barracks by the Japanese attack on Pearl Harbor as we trooped to the swimming pool. When we pointed out that this body of water had been built to train navy divers and, at 100 meters in length, was longer than anything we'd seen, our women's swim coach, Annelis Hoyman, reasoned that, if we could swim 100 meters, the 50 meters in Tokyo would seem quite short. At least swim practice got you excused from part of archery drill.

The scenery was pretty — as we rode through the dawn and the dusk to the practice venues. We even went through

Honolulu a couple of times. For our time off, we were sent to do a demonstration for the patients at Tripler Hospital. That trip, we got to see the cane fields and glimpses of the ocean from high viewpoints. The women team members enjoyed fan clubs. Young, male servicemen were what Hawaii had most of at the time. Our coaches didn't have a chance to carry the girls as we boarded the plane to fly to Tokyo. Our fan clubs of servicemen came to see us off and were more than happy to help us on the plane.

Olympic Village had been made totally accessible by the Japanese. There were some bad moments —like when we found the steepness of the ramp to the dining hall created a new Olympic event — and our top male athlete, Tim Harris, nearly decided to return immediately to the states when he discovered that public toilets in Japan were unisex.

Competitors were housed in real houses with six people per unit. "Damn!" one of my housemates exclaimed, "This thing is all girls!" "That won't last long," commented a voice from another room. "It will unless you find a way to get rid of me," replied our women's swim coach. With that, we broke records in unpacking and stowing our stuff and raced one another to the dining hall.

"Good Lord!" one of the men coaches grumbled as he extricated himself from a jam of wheelchairs as women from Britain, Ireland, Israel, Rhodesia, South Africa, the U.S. and other nations tried to outshout each other in an attempt to catch up on what had happened since they last met. "I can truly say I've experienced the Tower of Babel."

Those of us who had been in South Africa two years earlier were delighted to find the South African team leader was Alec Cooper, who, with his wife, Riki, had hosted Tom and

Louise Jones in Johannesburg. Alec's loyalties were stretched when I defeated the South African women's champ in three out of three swimming events. But he happily stood in for my coaches, Annelis and Stan, who were at other events, at the medals award ceremonies.

As in South Africa, all performances at the Paralympics were packed with spectators. Medals for Class IA women swimmers was first on the evening's agenda. When the announcer called out my name — which came out sounding like "Ritter-san" — over the public address system, I attacked the ramp to the winners' platform so fast that Alec held me back for fear I'd overshoot the platform and land on the Crown Princess of Japan, who would award the medal.

By my third trip to the top platform — one time each for backstroke, breaststroke and freestyle — the poor Crown Princess was in danger of being soaked by tears. Each time Old Glory went up the pole and the band played The National Anthem, I cried harder. This event was just too much for a kid from a farm in Wisconsin. I think the team was secretly relieved when I missed a gold in archery. We were all out of dry handkerchiefs.

I was exiled back to the press room to write releases for the newspapers back in the states for the remainder of the games. There was no star worship from the mostly male reporters with whom I shared the press room. They were more interested in getting me off one of the few typewriters we had so they could file their stories.

The USA won more gold medals than any other national team. Tim Harris succeeded in overcoming his Argentine rival. Jack Whitman, although he has significant paralysis in all four limbs, came within a few points of the international record for the grueling F.I.T.A. Round in archery — the record for able-bodied archers, that is. Records for the 100 meter dash by athletes using wheelchairs came within less than a second of able-bodied records, significant accomplishments for the equipment used in that time. Later, wheelchair runners would overturn NWAA regulations about configuration of racing wheelchairs and times for wheelchair dashes, 5,000 and 8,000 meter races and marathons would drop well below the time set by able-bodied runners.

Ben let us run around Toyko for a day after we finished the games. Stanley and I got lost and nearly missed the plane. The USA women's team fan club from Fort Derussey boarded our jet as we paused for fuel in Honolulu, bringing us leis of orchids and serenading us from the runway with the U. S. Army of the Pacific band.

chapter 16

My kind of town...

In 1966, with my master's degree completed and having traveled half the way around the world, the segment of the globe occupied by Champaign-Urbana was beginning to seem kind of small. The university community was actually, as Tim frequently pointed out, an artificial environment. People using wheelchairs had been, not only a common sight, but an integral part of the community for over 15 years. For residents of Champaign-Urbana, the fact that a person had a disability had become secondary to the fact that the person was on faculty at the university — like Dean Nosker, at the college of agriculture — or a university official — like Don Swift at the office of non-academic personnel — or a businessman — like Jack Whitman, in sales for WDWS radio, Lee Wise, in advertising for Eisner Food Company, or Tom Jones, sportscaster for WCIA-TV. Most churches, schools and neighborhood groups had somebody with a disability playing an active role.

Yet, people with disabilities had tackled the world beyond Champaign-Urbana and done well. Ben Graham and Ken Viste both had thriving medical practices, Dr. Graham, in the Pacific Northwest, and Dr. Viste, in Wisconsin. Both men had also had polio and were, functionally, paraplegics. Bob Arhelger and Will Johnson had taken their law degrees to California and not only practiced law, but had active roles in politics. Will had broken his neck in an accident and Bob had been born with cerebral palsy that prevented him from walking, using his hands for fine motions and speaking clearly.

When Bob and I had worked together while students, I traded my ability to type for Bob's insights on his field of study. Even that wasn't enough to get me an A in a political science course in grad school.

Could I do it? Could I make it in the outside world?

When I had been about 8 or 10 years old, the neighbor lady who lived on the farm across the road from ours had bundled up my Mother, my sister, Judy, and I and taken us to Chicago to see Marshall Fields at Christmas. Just because a kid lived on a farm 90 miles from Chicago shouldn't deprive them of that privilege — there were trains, weren't there? I fell in love with the town. Some day, I promised myself, Chicago would be my town.

Now was the day. After coaxing the 1956 Buick I'd bought for $600 up Routes 45 and 54 to the Big City on a couple of excursions to interview for public relations jobs in the suburbs, I got the break I needed. Art Wildhagen of the U of I Office of public relations and I had worked on many campus events together. Art thought I could write. Art knew that Chicago, as the industrial publishing capital of the country at that time, had hundreds of trade, business and professional magazines that needed writers — even if they did use wheels to get the job done. Off to Chicago again —

this time with some promising interviews lined up.

Chuck Flynn, the head of U of I public relations, greeted me at the recently opened Chicago Circle Campus of the U of I, built when the university decided to expand academic curricula beyond medical studies and a two-year selection of courses for which it had used Navy Pier. Chuck didn't have any openings at the time, but he knew a lot of people in the city. One was the publisher of The Chicago Tribune. To this day, I still wonder if I dreamed that I drove up to Michigan Avenue, found a place to park the car and caused a guard at Tribune Tower to think I was crazy when I told him I had an appointment with J. Howard Wood. He checked. I did. I recall being overwhelmed by being in his office and hearing him tell me that the Tribune might work me into their internal communications department. He also noted that the job would be a little boring and that he had a friend who headed the National Sporting Goods Association. NSGA was always looking for editors — and he liked the idea that the portfolio of sports articles I had shown did have some published by his own paper.

The publisher's directions about how to locate the corner of Wabash and Jackson were so good I found it on the first shot. Not only did Bob Goodwin, the publisher of NSGA's magazines, interview me and read my stories, he bought me lunch. Then he offered me a job as assistant editor on *Selling Sporting Goods*. I broke every rule of negotiating for a job. I told them the salary of $6,000 — twice what I was making at the U of I — was just great. I didn't even inquire about whether they would help with moving expenses and I asked if it would be too long if I took two weeks to clean up everything in Champaign and move to Chicago. Probably just as well. Writers were a dime a dozen in those days.

Back in Champaign, after they'd finished remarking about my obvious sudden attack of insanity, my buddies set about making sure I'd be in Chicago by the middle of December. Gibb found someone to sublease my apartment. Jack Whitman came up with a car that had been used by one of his fellow salesmen at WDWS — it was six years younger than the Buick, had tires with treads and brakes that worked every time you pushed down on the pedal — a real advance from the Buick. Then he talked the station into selling it for what I could afford. Freddy and Don, the infamous drivers of the U of I SRC buses, unloaded the Buick on some unsuspecting individual.

My apartment was furnished with items on loan from other grad students, who didn't have room for them in their places, a bed some other friends had removed from their mobile home, a remarkable desk created by sawing two discarded doors apart and nailing some two-by-fours on for legs and dozens of bricks and boards. The grad students moving into the apartment, both in wheelchairs, didn't have any more money than I did, so they gave me a few bucks. I gave them the furniture.

Edan Nicholas stuffed my car with clothing, the few dishes I owned, some books, an ironing board and my sewing machine. The last two were essential. Even though I would be making a fortune, I'd still have to make all my own clothes to save money. The couple of lamps I owned and a roll-away bed were stored at the SRC — by now located in a new building — until I could find a place to live in Chicago. Then, Carmie Blitz would haul them on a Greyhound bus to his shop in Chicago for repair.

Unfortunately, Edan and I were never ones to pay a lot of attention to details. The fact that the car was on the lawn in back of the apartment and it was raining hard didn't cause us any concern — until we tried to drive it across the lawn to the alley. Fortunately, there were a lot of big, male grad students living in the complex. In the years I'd lived there, we'd always cooperated — like, when we wanted a party, we'd each buy one ingredient needed to make ice cream and throw them in the ice-cream freezer we'd gone together to buy. The neighbor guys lifted the car our of the mud, the gals cheered and it was off to Chicago.

Of course, I was off to Chicago much later than planned, it was December and it was raining. It was raining too hard to see the roadsigns, but that was OK. The directions that my college friend, Marcia, had given me to locate her apartment on the near north side of the city weren't all that good anyway. My first encounter with the natives of Chicago taught me that attendants at service stations usually don't know that the street you're looking for is six blocks away.

Chicago was a lot different than Champaign —and a lot different than the experience I was relying on, gained from visiting my former roommates, Carol and Donna in Chicago. Carol lived in Riverdale and Donna, Oak Park. They didn't seem too much bigger than Champaign. They weren't. The Chicago Loop was.

Discoveries in the first few weeks included the fact that, if you held your breath while driving through traffic, you got dizzy. If you ventured out of the curb lane, you were likely to be run over by a couple hundred other drivers. If you stayed in the curb lane, you got squeezed by a CTA bus, and the cop that untangled the mess just handed you a piece of paper on how to get the CTA to repair the damages. The piece of paper could be summarized in two words — forget it.

Another discovery was that the city slogan, "Chicago Works," probably referred to the fact that "greasing the skids" was an effective way of getting along on many levels. "Greasing the skids" in Chicago covered everything from politicians lining up support among their constituents to folding a $10 bill around your driver's license when you handed it to a cop, who had been considering giving you a ticket. In my case, it was a way to find a place to live.

Marcia Hediger, a friend from college who had moved to Chicago to take a job as a counselor at one of the city's mental health centers, had invited me to stay with her while I located an apartment. We enjoyed each other's company and liked doing things together, however, the fact that we both used wheelchairs meant the traffic pattern in her one-bedroom apartment as we got ready to leave for work was a bit hard to handle. Phone calls following up on ads for apartments in the paper always seemed to reach the landlord just after the apartment had been rented. "For Rent" signs evidently were permanent fixtures that had meaning only if a tenant had departed earlier in the day.

Then, Marcia and I learned about the informal brotherhood of building engineers. Frank, the building engineer at Marcia's building, was drinking buddies with others who, after emigrating to the U.S. from Europe following WWII, had found work as "building engineers." They actually controlled most of the buildings on the mid-northside of Chicago. Frank introduced us to Henri, who didn't have a vacancy in his building either. After slipping Henri $20, I moved into

136

an efficiency apartment in his building the next week.

The builders of that four-plus-one apartment building had certainly been efficient. They'd crammed a living room/bedroom, bathroom and kitchen into a space 16 feet wide by 20 feet long — with three square feet left over for what they termed a foyer. For the year or more I lived in that apartment, I had to decide whether to get into bed on the side nearest the bathroom or on the side nearest the door, in case of fire. My hide-a-bed, when opened, didn't leave enough room to get by the end of the bed without folding it up first. The kitchen was a challenge. By taking the footrests off my chair, I could get to the stove and more-or-less reach into the sink. There wasn't enough room to get far enough into the kitchen to pass the refrigerator and open the door, so it was a matter of opening the door until it hit the side of my chair, then reaching back through the opening to retrieve food. When I moved, part of the clean-up effort revealed items of food that had slipped beyond my reach — and progressed through fuzzy with mold to fossilization.

The "Plus" in the term "Four Plus One" was the fact that the building stood on a pedestal so that the apartments on the second floor became the roof of the semi-enclosed parking area below. Parking was a definite plus in that area of the city. The other plus that came with this building was Henri. Henri immediately adopted any single female tenant who moved into his building. It was very handy for us when we wanted help moving something, or, in my case, needed a short, accessible path to the grocery store. Henri also knew which merchants would sell meat and produce, that had passed their maturity, at very low prices, how to arrange for a partially sheltered parking spot while paying only the "uncovered spot" rate and many, many more things to make life easier. In return, we offered Henri a pot of coffee and shelter when his wife went on the rampage and aimed every cooking utensil she owned at him when he stuck his head through the door. Despite the fact that Henri, when excited — which was most of the time — tended to speak a mixture of Belgian French, English and a few other languages, we understood him. We even understood the signs he taped to most of the vertical surfaces in the building saying such things as, "Dogs must not in the hallways," "Garbage should not do this," and "Tenants must by Tuesday" — all signed "Henri the eng."

Henri was a life-saver when it came to chipping your car out of a block of ice on any morning the temperature dropped below 15 degrees and the pipes in the part of the building which overhang the parking spaces burst. He also was a comfort as he stood and wrung his hands, moaning in god knows what language, every time thieves stole the batteries out of our cars, which also happened every time the temperature dropped below 15 degrees and the market for batteries got to be good for street entrepreneurs.

But the efforts were worth it. I moved to Chicago in December and the city was suddenly even more beautiful than I remembered from my visits as a child. At night, buildings had lights turned on in rooms so the pattern made the shape of Christmas trees. North Michigan Avenue twinkled with thousands of tiny white lights in the trees lining the sidewalks. And, the Christmas tree and window displays at Marshall Fields were even better than I remembered.

The people were nice, too. Curb cutouts in the Loop were not to appear for another 20 years, but I could jump most of the curbs. One exception was a 12" curb in an alley between my office and the Palmer House on Wabash. I hadn't decided how I was going to manage it as I headed one day, loaded with camera gear, to cover a story at the Palmer House. Four men, wearing the uniforms of an airline, were approaching and saw my hesitation — not difficult since I was perched on the edge of the curb, looking down in apprehension. They tipped their hats, said something in a foreign language, picked me and my chair up and carried me across the alley and set me gently on the opposite sidewalk. Which points up one change the Americans with Disabilities Act has made. We still don't have curb cutouts everywhere, but no person would give a hand like that for fear of being sued by the person in the wheelchair — as I found out 33 years later when I asked for assistance in a similar situation.

My salary seemed adequate when I took the job. After living on lima bean sandwiches while making $3,000 a year at the U of I, I was looking forward to at last being able to not have to choose between paying the car payments, eating or having a roof over my head. I didn't recall ever hearing, when I was at the U of I, about social security programs that supported people with disabilities. Tim Nugent probably would have killed us if we had heard and even briefly considered "welfare." Now, most of the few people I met who had disabilities lived on some type of public support.

I soon realized why. Having a disability is an expensive privilege. I had to rent an apartment in a building with an elevator. Other young writers, working at entry-level jobs lived in more spacious walk-up apartments in older, less expensive buildings. They rode the bus to work. I had to drive. Not only was there the insurance, gas and various licenses, the car had to be parked, which meant paying for parking at my apartment and at the office. My wheelchair had to have parts and service. I was overcharged several times before I found an honest wheelchair dealer.

These negatives were overcome by an intangible positive. Back then, before the laws were passed mandating that people in wheelchairs had to be protected and given equal opportunity, I found Chicago to have a natural system that supported me and made it possible for me to succeed.

One example of the people of Chicago was the group that ran the Apcoa Parking Garage near the corner of Wabash and Jackson. We liked each other the first day I showed up to park to go to the office. Looking at the posted rates for a monthly parking pass caused me to get dizzy — it was more than I had left in my budget for all incidentals and a few of the essentials. One of the car hikers explained to me that I qualified for a special rate — about half of the posted rate. It wasn't until years later that I learned that the men were paying part of my monthly parking pass out of their pockets. No insurance companies would issue insurance on cars driven with hand controls by people with disabilities. Yet, it was illegal to drive in Illinois without car insurance, so there was one choice — go into the insurance pool for uninsurable drivers and pay triple premiums. Not when my buddies at Apcoa found out. They happened to know this car dealer — who happened to kick all his business to an insurance company — who happened to owe him some favors. Results — insurance at the regular premium rate.

chapter 17

The intrepid editor

My job was really fun! Assistant editors were beyond the bottom of the totem pole in the publishing world. We were probably under the earth upon which the totem pole was resting. But I proof-read endless miles of galleys, wrote volumes of fillers that might never be used and happily played the role of gofer. At least the subject matter was fun. My experience writing wheelchair and some high school sports back at the university meant that I frequently knew more about the subjects than the male editors of the magazine, who were professional editors — not sports enthusiasts. I surprised them into letting me do some real stories by taking it in stride when they sent me out to do a story on a new sports cup, thinking I'd be embarrassed by something as risqué as a jockstrap. They tried telling me a cup was what you used to toast a winning team. I came back with some great information on protection of the male anatomy.

The guys liked me and were my friends, but they weren't above hazing the new kid. They told me it was an honor to handle the mechanical side of the magazine in addition to editorial. Somebody had to do it. NSGA was too cheap to hire a real production manager. As it turned out, they provided me with a unique education in publishing that was to make it possible for me to expand my skills — and future job opportunities.

The education was not without rough spots. It also wasn't long before I learned why I was being given this opportunity — and why, when I was looking for the job, people had said "NSGA is always looking for editors." It wasn't because we had a big magazine staff. It was because managing editors were considered by the company as the most expendable commodity. These guys were apparently hired so there would be someone handy to fire if the magazine was late or if the advertising load dropped or if he went crazy and edited some words out of the executive director's column. Occasionally, the association would slip up and hire a new managing editor before firing the present one, but not often.

Not only did the guy that hired on as managing editor have to learn more than humanly possible just to get the next issue out, he had to deal with the politics of a trade association. People in the editing trade have a good grapevine. They knew which houses treated managing editors well — and which ones used managing editors as cannon fodder. We were at the head of the cannon fodder list. We got the guys who were either shaky editors or had crawled all the way into a bottle along the way. I remember one managing editor sitting at his desk and sobbing until the other guys hauled him away. Another one routinely took a two-hour, six martini lunch and his copy in the afternoon was a little too esoteric to publish.

The good part was that I was the one who got to go to the

press and put the magazine to bed. First I found out what press we were using that month. Then I found out where Rochelle, Illinois was — not awfully near Chicago, it turned out. When I arrived at the plant, the second-shift foreman — after calling NSGA to confirm that this was really what they'd sent out as an editor — told me that our magazine had slots for two 32-up, four-color forms on his shift. Was I ready? Ready for what? To me, a slot was a long, narrow opening in something. 32-up could have been a super powerful soft drink for all I knew. I did know about four-color. It was what the managing editors swore at when they tried to lay out a magazine.

The foreman muttered something about girls not belonging in printing plants. He didn't even get to the part about the wheelchair. But, he was a proud old craftsman. Evidently, he considered me a challenge to his mastery of his craft and his reputation for always getting the magazine out. Seeing my blank look as he tossed the press layout forms on the desk I'd taken in the editors' room, he sighed, led me to his office and started at the beginning.

"When we print magazines, we print in increments of four pages at a time. Since you're running over 200 pages this month, we're going to put you on the four-color Heidelberg press. She can handle 32 pages-up at a time. You turn the sheet over, print 32 pages on back and you have a 64-page signature for folding and gathering to be bound into the book. Now, on this layout sheet, you see that the pages aren't in consecutive order — see, they're more in a spiral so that page 14 ends up on the back of page 13 when you're done."

He must have thought I was getting all of this because he

continued, "These markings are for each channel. All of your 4-A colors have to be in separate channels. You can't put 4-A red and 4-A blue in the same channel — unless you're after mud brown. Matched colors can't be in the same channel with 4-A colors — or any other color unless you're sure they're the same match from the same advertiser. See these marks? That's where the grippers hit as they hold the form on the press. Any type in that area is smashed — so no bleeds under the grippers." At least I knew that a bleed is when the engraving ran through the margin to the edge of the page.

The lesson went on far into the night. By the time the magazine was put to bed, I understood a lot about letterpress printing. And I sure knew that if you missed your "slot" — the time set for forms in your magazine to be run— you went to the bottom of the list and the magazine didn't get out on time. I would spend a lot of time in printing companies in the next five years. The constant challenge of getting all the pages in a form cleared so the form could run, being able to write something at the last minute to fill three empty inches on a page or how to replace a page of advertising — when the engraving didn't arrive by air freight — helped train a person to handle the unexpected.

I wasn't the only one who didn't expect the amount of snow that arrived on January 26, 1967. The entire city of Chicago was unprepared. In keeping with the "magazine must go through" philosophy, NSGA executives refused to believe the reports of a blizzard being brought in, first by people who'd been outside, then by our delivery people calling in to say their trucks were mired in snow. The rest of the building was deserted when we finally were allowed to leave at 4:00 p.m. I was able to struggle the few yards from the door of 23 E. Jackson to the lobby of DePaul University. From there, I was able to make it to the parking garage with the help of some of the few pedestrians left on the street.

A few parking attendants remained, settled in for the night, it seemed. They refused to bring my car down from the garage, saying, "It's too dangerous out there — the Shore Drive is closed — there are cars stuck everywhere — you'd freeze to death in the car."

The alternative seemed to be freezing to death in the ticket booth of the parking garage until one of the attendants noticed a Chicago police squad car inching along Wabash. Somehow, with a great deal of arm waving and shouting from what I could see, the garage attendant finally convinced one of the officers to leave his squad and find out what the emergency was. His response, upon seeing me was, "What do you want me to do? What's this broad doing out in a blizzard in a wheelchair anyway?"

The garage attendants argued that the police might be able to get me to the YMCA hotel down the street where I could at least find shelter. The cop argued that it was illegal to carry a civilian in a police car unless they were under arrest. Then, the garage attendants, reasoned, arrest me for cluttering up their garage — do anything. Finally, the cop's partner, whose squad was stuck in one place anyway, wandered over to see what the fuss was about. The garage attendants won. Four men carried my chair and me over the snow. It took an hour and a half for the two officers to negotiate the five blocks of snarled traffic before they carried me across the snow into the lobby of the YMCA hotel.

The hotel thought they were full. The police assured them

they weren't. The next day was a strange party as a group of strangers got to know one another in our snow-enforced prison. The selection of food offered by the hotel got pretty weird by the second day, but by then, some of us were able to walk down the deserted streets and and bum some food at the Art Institute. The Institute had food, but no visitors — and the staff stranded there seemed to be glad to see some new faces.

Several days after the storm had struck, the city managed to get at least one lane open on most streets and clear enough of the cars off Lake Shore Drive for me to make my way to my apartment. The garage attendants had predicted correctly. More than a few of the cars uncovered after the storm held the bodies of those who had frozen to death. I was only able to drive as far as the parking lot of the food store a quarter of a block from my apartment. However, Henri, the eng, had alerted the neighborhood to my disappearance and I was spotted as soon as I got the chair out of the car. Neighborhood men rushed out with shovels and, half digging paths, half carrying the chair over the snow, they soon had me in my apartment. One of the men even had thought to bring some of the few groceries the store had left.

The snow was followed by sub-zero cold and it seemed that I had yet to prove that I could deal with a variety of challenges presented by life in the big city. It also seemed that the big city saved up quite a variety of events with which to deal.

Each year, NSGA held one of the largest trade conventions in the city, the show at which sporting goods dealers from across the country ordered their supply of products for the spring, summer and fall sales seasons. The guys on the staff had warned me that covering McCormick Place, the exhibition center where the conference was held, would be a challenge.

McCormick Place was the most advanced of any exhibition center in the country at the time. Display space was measured in acres. Semi-trailer trucks were swallowed by the halls when they pulled in to unload exhibits. Hundreds of people were employed at the decorating companies, drayage services, restaurants and other services housed in the center. Not only was McCormick Place totally modern, it was totally fireproof. No chance that baby could burn. It was totally steel and concrete.

About two weeks before the NSGA show was to open, the top item on the radio morning news as I got ready to leave for work was, "the Chicago fire department has brought the blaze at McCormick Place under control — the entire building is said to be a total loss."

It was a novel introduction to being part of the management of a major trade show. For once, the magazine staff had been prepared ahead of time and most of the printed materials for the show were done. We started over, dumped the covers for the 300-page show issue of the magazine and ran a new one with a photo of the fire superimposed across the painting of McCormick Place we had commissioned. We also threw out the match books with the painting of McCormick on the cover, which we'd neatly overprinted with "Set Your Sales on Fire!"

The destruction of McCormick Place had made all of the work by the magazine department invalid. Not only was each exhibitor's booth number at McCormick Place listed in the magazine, but also in a 300-page show directory.

The editorial staff packed a few clothes and moved to the press in Waukegan, Illinois to work 'round the clock to change the magazine and show directory. This was complicated by the fact that the NSGA sales staff were frantically running around Chicago, arranging booth space at Navy Pier, the Conrad Hilton, The Palmer House — and anywhere else they could find replacement display space for well over 1,000 booths.

It was a worn-out group of editors who arrived back at Navy Pier to help cheer up our exhibitors as they moved in to set up their displays. Their general crankiness originated because many had lost their exhibits in the fire because they'd been stored in the lower storage areas of McCormick Place. Others knew their exhibits were somewhere in the Midwest, but because of the blizzard, trucking companies were frequently unable to pinpoint the location of their trucks. The exhibitors' unhappiness level rose sharply when the Chicago Fire Department — having been much more severely burned by the press than McCormick Place had been by the fire — decided that escape exits must be open adjacent to the exhibit area during the entire set-up. This was possible. At one time in its multi-purposes life, Navy Pier was a commercial shipping dock.

The amount of wind and 10-degree temperature that could come through the truck doors spaced along the Pier nearly blew everyone, including the fire department, off into Lake Michigan. The cold didn't work as a means to cool down tempers that rose by the hour. Drayage men screamed at decorators. Exhibitors screamed at us. Truck drivers and cops screamed at each other and everyone screamed in unison when the Chicago Fire Department accidently set fire to the carpeting in a huge booth while conducting a burn test. It seemed that fire code didn't really intend for a butane lighter to be held against the material until it finally ignited. At least the lake was just outside the door and the fire was extinguished when the carpeting was dumped overboard.

This show was my first clue that working a trade show using a wheelchair has its challenges. The coated handrims on my wheelchair caused blisters on my fingers after a couple of runs up and down the half-mile length of the Pier. But, there were rewards. The editors doubled in press relations and we got to arrange interviews with the stars, who were appearing at the show to promote various sporting goods. I had my picture taken with Tom Tyron, who'd just starred in Winchester 73, and was promoting Winchester rifles. The best thing was that my hero, Bart Starr, quarterback of my team — the Green Bay Packers — actually talked to me. He wanted directions to somewhere — but it was still a conversation.

The show came off despite the problems. We weren't surprised that pilferage of exhibitors' goods reached an all time high. Security was hampered by the show being spread over so many places, the city's concern about fire and public safety and the pressure of last-minute arrangements. We always wondered, though, how someone managed to walk out of the Palmer House carrying a full size, slate bedded billiard table.

The blizzard and the show gave me confidence that a kid in a wheelchair could make it in the big city. I used that confidence when the next managing editor disappeared. When I announced that I wanted to move up to managing editor — since I was handling the duties between managing editors —

which was most of the time, the publisher explained life to me; women aren't managing editors unless the magazine is a woman's magazine. I told him I'd quit. He told me he'd accept my resignation. I put an ad in the "Positions Wanted" section of the Tribune and moved to another magazine. The company who hired me published magazines in such fascinating areas as food chemistry and manufacturing, cosmetic chemistry and detergents and surfactants formulations. My best work was a three-part series on the effect of the sexual cycles of cocoa capsids on the cocoa commodities market. It turned out that the little capsid bugs got hornier than usual at certain intervals and ate huge portions of the cocoa crop before it could be harvested, which in turn blew the New York Commodity Exchange away. Well, it was a way I could earn enough to pay the rent.

The job at the publishing company was also boring. That was good because it left me with enough creativity and energy to do some free-lancing in the evenings and on weekends. The income from free-lancing was enough to replace the car that I'd bought in Champaign with a new Chevy. The poor old car had over 90,000 miles on it and, according to one mechanic, would soon drop its transmission — probably in the middle of the Eisenhower Expressway.

In the early '70's, we didn't have the services for people with disabilities that later developed. In this instance, my new car needed hand controls. The one guy in the Chicago area who installed them, himself in a wheelchair, was in the hospital and out of commission for who knew how long. Another company that installed hand controls was in Rockford, Illinois, which meant the car dealer would have to have one of his people drive the car to Rockford, return to Chicago and go get the car when it was done. One of the dealer's mechanics looked at the hand controls on the old car and said he thought he could figure out how to switch them over to the new car.

He came pretty close to getting it right. The car drove OK when we tested it on the suburban streets around the dealership. The part he didn't get right showed up when I tried to accelerate to merge into traffic on the Eisenhower Expressway. It seems that the rod that sleeved into the hollow tube that depressed the accelerator was a little too long, so our friendly mechanic did the logical thing — cut some of it off. This remedy worked until the hand control lever was pushed down far enough to cause the rod to slip out of the hollow tube. This action resulted in total loss of communication between the driver and the accelerator. For the record, cars will creep along on their own long enough to get off an expressway and onto a side street, where a girl with any mechanical ability can reconnect the rod and the tube. Also for the record, driving 15 miles on the Eisenhower at a speed of 20 miles per hour results in a lot of other motorists honking their horns, shaking their fists and exhibiting generally poor manners.

chapter 18

Action for and by the people with disabilities

When I moved to Chicago, I had intended to concentrate on a career in journalism and leave activities revolving around people with disabilities behind. Wasn't being a role model and example of how a person with a disability could handle a job enough?

However, a bunch of the guys who had been on the USA wheelchair teams with me had also moved to Chicago. They gave great parties. By the end of one of those parties, I'd volunteered to help with the National Wheelchair Basketball Tournament being held in Chicago in the spring. My former teammates and I had graduated with college degrees, gotten good jobs and become responsible members of our communities. We hadn't, it seems, improved our ability to coordinate events to any degree higher than it had been when we lost parts of the Illinois Gizz Kids on the way to games.

This time, we lost three entire basketball teams when Bruce and I forgot to put some streets — that turned out to be critical turning points — on the maps we gave out to the tournament participants. Two of the teams took their extended tour of Chicago and suburbs pretty well. The St. Louis Rams, who had transferred their intense rivalry with the Illinois Gizz Kids to the Chicago Sidewinders, claimed that we'd left the streets off the maps on purpose so the Sidewinders would have an advantage in the finals. The argument was settled in typical NWBA fashion. The guys all went out drinking together after the game and a Ram stole one of the Sidewinders player's artificial leg and hid it. It took the Chicago team half the next morning to find it.

Enough of organizing events, said I, let George do it. As coincidence would have it, George was doing it. My close buddy from U of I and Africa, George Conn, was chairman of the committee to plan the first independent conference of the National Paraplegia Foundation. George and I often went out to dinner. At the end of one of those dinners, it seemed only polite to agree to be George's co-chairman for the conference. After all, George paid for dinner.

The National Paraplegia Foundation was one of the first organizations to be run by people with disabilities, rather than run for people with disabilities by caretakers, as was the case with organizations like United Cerebral Palsy and the Muscular Dystrophy Association. The organization of NPF was nurtured by another group of people with disabilities, the Paralyzed Veterans of America — PVA.

Not too long after the end of WWII, paralyzed veterans had grown tired of being treated as perpetual patients by the Veterans Administration. PVA had some wheelchair sports teams, but they also focused on better care and support of federal legislation to provide paralyzed veterans with more adequate benefits. The men who founded PVA were both innovative and energetic. If the public wanted to show sympathy for the disabled vets, they could buy the greeting cards PVA sold. If there was no decent wheelchair repair service in New York, PVA would start its own business. If congressmen needed prodding to advance veterans' benefits, PVA prodded. In a relatively short time, PVA had established chapters across the nation.

Some of the PVA members, including Jim Smittkamp and Bob Moss, felt that civilians with disabilities needed an organization that gave them a coordinated voice, so the National Paraplegia Foundation was established. From the stories told by Jim Smittkamp, who became executive director of NPF, the group tended to consider PVA as its benefactor, fairy godmother and a few other things that would provide money and services. There were some hints that the civilians with disabilities felt that the veterans, with their pensions and other benefits, had it much easier than disabled people without service connections and it was OK to let PVA carry NPF as long as PVA would. In the late '60's and early '70's, PVA began hinting strongly that NPF should grow up and stand on its own. They made those hints stronger by suggesting that NPF organize and hold its own conference, and separate from PVA in 1970. Knowing the PVA guys, they probably put up part of the money to hold the conference.

That first conference was what NPF needed to bring members together and excite them with the possibilities offered by the organization. The first conference, held in Hillside, Illinois, had scientific presentations on spinal cord injury and other disabilities, peer discussion groups, sports demonstrations and exhibits of equipment and services for people with disabilities. Most of those with disabilities who attended had strenuously avoided joining any group that was sponsored for the good of disabled people. Having fought hard for their independence and an image of capability, they didn't want to be herded into activities that well-intentioned able-bodied people thought were appropriate for the disabled.

Working together to account for all of the details necessary to bring off a conference of this size had resulted in most of us overlooking each other's disabilities. John Schleicher, whose paralysis from a cervical spinal cord injury had been complicated by some medical treatment that went wrong, summed it up with the idea that these are neat people who you really could be friends with — even if they were crips. John, who with his wife, Joanne, owned a printing company in Rockford, didn't like a lot of other crips. He preferred to lure beautiful young ladies within reach with his husky whisper — also a result of a bit of ill-planned medical treatment — and flirt. Joanne shrugged and compared him to their little dog, who chased cars, but never drove away in any he caught.

John became a group leader in shocking members of the medical profession and the public into seeing that a person with a severe disability has all the characteristics and goals as any other citizen randomly selected from a crowd. He once left three-quarters of an audience of nurses in helpless laughter with his blow-by-blow description of how to change an indwelling catheter in a home setting. The remaining quarter of the audience was shocked into silence by his comparison of using talcum powder to prevent abrasion as "just like rolling a piece of chicken in flour before you fry it."

His accomplice in such activities was frequently Ellen Daly, a Milwaukee housewife and mother of five. Ellen, although a paraplegic as a result of a rare neurological condition — the name of which I couldn't spell if I could remember it — thought nothing of throwing some or all of the kids in her van and driving to some other city to hold a meeting. She once had to reorganize a conference in three days when some citizens of Milwaukee talked the city council into believing that the meeting, focusing on developing a healthy sex life after incurring a disability, was too risque to be held within the city limits. Ellen found a suburban location just in time and the meeting was held.

The citizens of Milwaukee were not the only ones who felt it was pretty indecent to think people with disabilities could still want an active sex life. More than one man in his early 20's was told that he and his wife would have to take up some other activity — possibly Chinese checkers — by his medical advisors. In fact, this was the routine counseling practiced in major rehabilitation centers.

Perhaps, this line of thinking wasn't so unusual. Sex is for adults. It's not hard to get into a habit of thinking of people with disabilities as less than true adults. Children can walk at about the age of 18 months. People with disabilities can't. Children can control their bowels and bladders at about two years. People with spinal cord injury, multiple sclerosis and other disabilities frequently can't. Children can dress and feed themselves at a rather early age. People paralyzed from the neck down can't. You wouldn't expect a three year old to have sexual intercourse, would you?

The medical authorities knew that spinal cord injury frequently resulted in men being unable to have what the doctors considered a normal erection. Women with spinal cord injuries couldn't feel their lower bodies anyway, so why bother. These theories were proved invalid by the number of women who became pregnant by their spinal-cord-injured husbands and the number of spinal-cord-injured women who delivered healthy babies.

Not all doctors bought the idea that the idea — or even the topic — of sex was taboo in rehabilitation. Of course, a lot of their colleagues thought Ted Cole, M.D., and his wife, Sandra, were on the verge of being pornographers when they created a series of clinical films of consenting adults with spinal cord injuries, cerebral palsy and other disabilities engaged in sex with their partners. The films were straightforward and tastefully done. The Coles used them not only for the education of people with disabilities, but to teach healthcare professionals who worked with the disabled not to be shy of the topic. At a couple of conventions, you had to sneak to their rooms to review their work because convention organizers weren't ready for this breakthrough — humanizing the patient, indeed!

Not a lot of rehab centers bought the practice of Craig Rehabilitation Hospital in Denver, Colorado, either. Bob Jackson, M.D., insisted that newly injured patients at Craig have the opportunity to explore their options for sex with their wives and husbands — or an interested close friend. He even provided locked, very private rooms for that rehabilitation treatment activity.

We believed Bob Jackson when he told us he'd served in a M.A.S.H. unit in Korea. Hawkeye Pierce could have learned a few tips from Bob. When he headed Craig, the hospital certainly felt like the set of the TV show, M.A.S.H. Dr. Jackson forbade his staff to wear the white or grey lab coats so dear to the hearts of the medical profession. As a matter of fact, most of the physical and occupational therapy ladies wore hot pants to work. Instead of the patients being dressed by aides and taken to the therapy treatment area to learn to get dressed, as was the practice in many rehab centers, the patients at Craig got up and got dressed, then went to one of the two open floors — no treatment cubicles — where patients worked on what they thought would help them most. If you wanted to lift weights for two hours, you lifted weights for two hours. If you wanted to sit in the hall all day, it seemed you could do so. You probably wouldn't have a very long stay at Craig if you did.

After meeting Bob Jackson through NPF, I would visit Craig on many occasions through the years as part of my jobs. If possible, you scheduled a trip at Halloween, when all Craig staff members and people who routinely entered the hospital — like service and delivery people — had to be in costume for the day. One year, when the head of nursing — who could have led a regiment of Marines if she'd chosen — had her staff appear in outfits worn by prostitutes in Denver when the town was in its heyday, Jackson, not to be outdone, called the Colorado state police, made a deal and had the entire nursing staff hauled off in squad cars for soliciting.

Dr. Jackson and his closest physician-in-crime, John Young, M. D., had started Craig. Young had gone on to develop a rehabilitation center similar to Craig at Good Samaritan Hospital in Phoenix, AZ when the two of them attached themselves to NPF. They were a good addition. It was never boring with Jackson and Young around. At one meeting,

Jackson had room service wake Young up for a huge meal at 3:30 a.m. — after a rather strenuous night of party conducting. Young retaliated by stuffing towels in the toilet in Jackson's room so that Jackson almost had to swim for the door in the middle of the next night.

Jackson and Young were the first doctors many of us in NPF with disabilities had as close friends. They weren't always playing pranks. Bob Jackson's presentations usually centered on the contention that the rehabilitation process taught people to be disabled. If a person without a disability were locked up in an institution for six to nine months, having everything from blowing his nose to changing his pants done for him, Jackson maintained, that perfectly able person would emerge having learned helplessness. Bob raised a lot of young doctors that spread his philosophy. Although he died young — in his 50's — there are several rehab centers around the country that still practice Jacksonian theory. Get the person back into the mainstream of life as soon as possible — like their second day in the hospital.

Young made sense. One of his lectures that impressed me the most was about the choice a person with a disability had to make. He'd look at me and say, "would you rather spend five days a week going to physical therapy and hoping some day you'd walk or would you rather do like you are doing — chase men and make people's lives miserable with your demands for better wheelchairs and stuff. "There comes a point," he would continue, "when you have to say to yourself, this is how I am. Now what am I going to do with it."

Dr. Young also delighted in destroying the myth that people with disabilities are wonderfully patient individuals endowed with courage, lofty ideals and all that sort of nonsense that people like to believe. "If some drunken SOB gets his spinal cord severed in a knife fight," Young would say, "he's going to be a drunken SOB in a wheelchair. Disability does not result in personality change nor sainthood."

Like Jackson, Dr. Young left a legacy in many ways. One was his work to establish a network to record and study incidents of spinal cord injury across the nation. Prior to his work in the 1970's, no one knew how many people sustained spinal cord injuries, how they became injured, their age, sex or occupation. Maybe, since most insurance companies still listed the life expectancy of people with spinal cord injuries in single-digit numbers of years, no one thought it was important.

NPF, although perpetually on the brink of financial insolvency, grew well following the first convention. This was a result of commitment on the part of people with disabilities. It's doubtful that Jim Smittkamp, executive director of the national office in Chicago, ever cashed a paycheck. He probably didn't even bother having one issued. Soon there were chapters in over a dozen states. Each chapter was run and financed by people with disabilities. Chapters scorned the use of cute little kids, struggling on crutches, to raise money — but they did everything else. You didn't escape from a chance meeting with a member of the Milwaukee chapter without having ordered a case of salted nuts, for example.

In addition to family and peer counseling, NPF chapters took on the community. One of our fun events in Chicago involved having celebrities use wheelchairs for a day and try to get around Chicago's Loop. Greg Landry, quarterback of the Detroit Lions at the time, did very well. He even learned to jump curbs. Bobby Douglass, quarterback of the Chicago Bears, got his wheelchair stuck in the back seat of his car and we had to loan him another chair for the photo opportunities. One Chicago alderman fell off a curb in his chair, which influenced him to change his vote in city council to support curb cuts. Channel 7 TV loved it — a story about people in wheelchairs that wasn't intended to tug heartstrings.

Our network in NPF was also the source of an instant nucleus of fire-fighters when the need arose — like when the FAA decided in the mid-70's to ban people dependent on wheelchairs from commercial flights. There was also the possibility that anyone using a wheelchair would have to buy a ticket for an attendant or be denied the right to fly. Such a ruling would have cost many of us our jobs since we used airplanes to get to meetings, sales calls and other work activities.

Airline travel in a wheelchair, even before this new threat, was chancy at best. Most of us who traveled much could relate stories of being stranded in a strange city when the airline with which we were connecting would refuse to fly us. I was more fortunate than most in that, living in Chicago, I could use United Airlines. Not only did they let people in wheelchairs fly, they hired people with disabilities as executives of the company.

So, we gathered the NPF forces and some buddies from PVA and fought for our rights at the hearing. I don't think the FAA officials had expected the people who were about to be banned to show up ready to argue their own case. They got funny looks on their faces when one of us pointed out that the FAA's reasoning for banning us — we couldn't get out of the airplane quickly if it crashed — was pretty invalid. In those days, no one got out of a plane if it crashed. They were all dead. Besides, an NFL linebacker couldn't evacuate if he were knocked unconscious. Finally, PVA lost their patience, sent a group of their members who were paralyzed out to an FAA test site and demonstrated that they could crawl out just as fast as the other passengers.

The FAA relented. We could fly if the airline crew had no objections. This was close to equal. The pilot can always refuse a passenger if he feels the passenger's inebriation, hostility or other behavior would threaten the comfort and safety of other passengers. Most airlines were pretty easy to work with.

And then there was Eastern. I never flew Eastern if I could avoid it, but one time I was headed for Puerto Rico from Washington, DC and Eastern was the only carrier. My ticket was invalid, the Eastern Airline people told me, unless I could get permission to fly signed by my doctor not more than 24 hours prior to the flight. Good. My doctor was in Chicago. It was then I found out what congressional aides are good for — beating up airlines and getting an exception to the rule. Being on a congressional advisory panel, it was not hard for me to get an aide to trot out to National airport and get Eastern to set aside the policy in this instance.

If you can't beat them, win them over. By the mid-1970's, I had a job — which is another chapter in this work — that required flying frequently. I discovered that the first rule to follow for no-hassle flying was to not follow the airlines' rules. Airlines tell you to call in advance and make arrangements if you use a wheelchair. For first-time travelers or people with power chairs, this is a good rule. For someone whose living depends on flying around the country, it's a lousy rule.

First, the airline wanted to meet you at the curb, take your own wheelchair away and put you in something that no one could push, was always too big for your body, had a seat that would guarantee a pressure sore in half an hour and wouldn't fit in an airport toilet stall. The last part was a moot point anyway, because after the airline people put you in their chair, they parked you in a spot in the airport marked FOR PEOPLE WITH PROBLEMS until time to board the flight. Then, they took your chair and threw it in with the freight. When you got where you were going, you had to be hauled to the baggage area to claim the parts of what had been your wheelchair.

For several months, a ticket agent — who was determined to follow the rules to the letter — and I played a game. I eluded him the first time he tried to take my personal chair at the ticket counter. He followed me, but lost me that trip. The next week, when I appeared again, he found someone to cover his station and gave chase. An ultra-light racing wheelchair can be propelled faster than a person can run, as proven by the times of marathon runners using wheelchairs versus marathon runners using their legs. I wasn't a marathon runner, but neither was the ticket agent. In fact, he tended to get out of breath after about the length of four gates. Several times that summer, we provided entertainment for passengers waiting for planes as he and I raced down good old concourse E.

Making friends with gate agents and crews proved a very effective way of assuring an enjoyable flight. Arriving at the gate unannounced resulted in having time for some friendly conversation with the gate agent. My chair traveled in the cabin or the special luggage compartment long before ADA and recent changes in airline policies. Usually, the gate agent got so interested in talking about what I did for a living, that he or she would decide it would be easier to assign me to the first seat in first class. Then we didn't have to mess around with a transfer chair. That seat meant that I got to be friends with a lot of crews.

Crews have a lot of pull. I once arrived at O'Hare to find that, because United was having big ceremonies to launch their 767 plane, our plane had to unload using the portable stairs. Anyone who has ever been carried down a flight of portable stairs on a transfer chair can tell you that you're positive you're going to end up embedded in the tarmac at the bottom. Airline crews don't like this duty anymore than the passenger.

This crew was innovative. They brought my chair to me, pulled a forklift up to the food galley bay and I pranced onto the forklift in my chair. The forklift driver and the United ground crewman conferred and came to the conclusion that I'd never find my way through the bowels of O'Hare if they let me in a door on the lower level. It didn't take them long to get a friendly gate agent on their communications device. He had a gate open. We trundled across the apron, the forklift driver raised the platform to gate level and I sneaked into the terminal. They probably didn't clear this act with headquarters. They probably would have been given mental health leave if they'd tried.

Federal legislation has mandated access to public transportation, but a lot of the progress made in the earlier days was because individuals listened and acted. In addition to the curb cutouts and accessible entrances brought about by the efforts of NPF, one change brought about by Access Living, of Chicago, certainly made air travel more comfortable for those of us who used both O'Hare and wheelchairs.

Access Living is a group of people with disabilities who formed the organization to help others with disabilities achieve independent living. Although Access Living has many accomplishments in the areas of promoting accessibility in housing and public transportation, my personal favorite thing they accomplished concerned the matter of someone in a wheelchair using a bathroom at O'Hare. There was no way to use a toilet on an airplane in those days, so a lot of times, one arrived at O'Hare after a four- or five-hour flight with a real urge to go. In order to do so, you had to locate the first aid station, then you had to fill out a form telling the nurse why you had to go to the bathroom. By the time you got through the paperwork, it could have been too late.

The leaders at Access Living had friends in high places — like the assistant to the commissioner of aviation for the city of Chicago. She claims she threatened to lock him out of his private toilet until accessible stalls were put in the public toilets along each concourse. The commissioner, who later became a good friend of mine, denies he needed such prodding. Which ever story is correct, O'Hare had wheelchair accessible toilets before any government regulations mandated them.

Maybe the ADA was the result of such ground work by individuals and groups of people who have disabilities. Maybe the legislation wouldn't have been needed if more friendly discussions had been held between authorities of both the public and private sector and people with disabilities. It could have even resulted in using common sense.

chapter 19

Smoke 'n' mirrors

Development of certain products — called assistive tech-nology — has helped make it possible for people with disabilities to achieve success in getting an education, per-forming on the job or being more active in the community. Again, I had the privilege of being there when some of these products were developed and being a close observer at the birth of others. As with the opportunities gained by the dis-abled in education, employment and access to public facili-ties, there are a lot of people who played a part in develop-ing these products. Some of them had disabilities. Some did not. Most of the time, the disabled and nondisabled worked together. Sometimes, they didn't.

My observation post from which to see the development of wheelchairs which assisted, rather than deterred, the user, individualized seating for wheelchairs, electronic communi-cations for those who could not talk and much, much more was with a company called Medical Equipment Distributors, Inc. — MED.

MED was organized in 1969 by five men who had built excellent businesses that delivered oxygen and home care equipment — like hospital beds and commodes — to people at home so they could recuperate under the care of their families. What these guys liked best, though, was working with people, whose disabilities were permanent, to see how various equipment could help them solve their problems. In 1969, these men — Lewie Bates, Jr., in Greenville, South Carolina; Nagle Bridwell, in Philadelphia; Frank Jones, in Indianapolis, Indiana, and Dewey Kuhn, in Minneapolis, Minnesota were convinced by Bob Kruse and Chuck Chevillon, who operated a similar business in Chicago, that they could protect their businesses from being taken over by some giant companies — with names like Sears, Hertz and Abbey — who had decided medical equipment was a profitable area.

They formed MED. For a while, MED was just a group of guys from around the country who got together a couple of times a year to share problems and solutions. Then, in 1970, somebody in the group got the idea that, if MED were to issue a catalog, each company could increase its sales and services. Kruse and Chevillon had already done much work on a catalog for their company, AAMED, but — with the unselfishness that was the trademark of the group in those early days — the two Chicagoans offered to share their work with the others.

Chevillon remembered that one of his most-difficult-to-please customers was some kind of a journalist. He'd learned that when she'd chewed him out about her wheelchair breaking just when she needed to go to Hammond, Indiana to cover a story. Chevillon wasn't quite sure what the woman did, but surely, if she claimed she was a journalist, she could handle a little thing like a catalog. The customer was me. Chuck hired me on the spot. I wasn't quite sure what MED was — or what kind of catalog they had in mind — or what I'd be paid. Actually, I thought it was going to be a free-lance job.

Chuck Chevillon was typical of the men who had founded MED. He took a personal interest in all of his customers who had long-term disabilities. I had found that out when I went into AAMED to buy a new wheelchair. The one I had been using since college had shed most of its chrome and developed bad deformities caused by bends in the frame. Since I wasn't on any type of public assistance, buying a new one myself was the only option — and it had taken me a long time to save the $500 for that new chair. I'd been ripped off by dealers for repairs to the chair. I wasn't going to let that happen when I bought a new chair. "On the defensive" didn't even start to describe my attitude toward Chuck when he came out to wait on me.

For a while, we sparred. I told him that I not only knew every vice president Everest & Jennings had, but I also knew the president of the company, Gerald Jennings — so don't try to rip me off, buddy. Chevillon replied with accounts of how he also knew everyone at E & J — including the late Mr. Everest, for whom the original Mr. Jennings had designed the first folding wheelchair. Not only that, he personally prescribed most of the wheelchairs at Chicago's two rehabilitation centers. I countered with my personal experiences of being over-charged and poorly served by dealers.

This went on until Chevillon played an ace. He pointed out that the chair I was using was much too large for me. Someone of my tall, slender build should be in a narrow wheelchair. That did it. Any time you tell a woman she has a small ass, it takes all her arguments away. He even offered me the same discount he would have given to a state agency.

The wheelchair he sold me soon presented the opportunity to get to know this man much better. Before E & J had gained most of the market in wheelchairs because of the lack of competition, all of their chairs had been carefully handcrafted by master welders. By the early 1970's, the demand was so great that the company had moved to assembly line production. They also were trying to respond to the demand of dealers like Chevillon by trying new features on the chairs.

It would be another 15 years before any wheelchair company grasped the concept of field-testing new features. The manufacturer simply added new parts or features to the chair, sent it out the door and hoped they didn't get calls. They didn't get many because, first, most dealers didn't have very close contact with their customers and, second, who would listen to a customer anyway?

The first thing to go on my new chair were the tires. A new rim design allowed the innertube to sneak between the tire and the rim. This, of course, cut the innertube, causing a loud explosive noise. My fellow employees at the publishing company thought they were being shot at. I nearly jumped off the Eisenhower Expressway when a tire exploded right behind me in the back seat of my car.

The wheel rim problem got solved. Then E & J decided to make the wheel locks prettier. Wheel locks consist of a lever that pushes a piece of metal against the tire and holds the chair in place while you transfer to the car — or toilet or wherever. Wheel locks also keep your chair from rolling backward when you reach for things on your desk, for example. E & J decided to enclose the wheel locks in a pretty, chrome plated box with the logo stamped on it. The only function the box served was to keep you from noticing that the spring mechanism had slipped out of place. The spring slipping out place resulted in me landing in the mud while trying to transfer into my car and, on another occasion, meeting a really cute Royal Canadian mounted policeman when the wheel lock failing dumped me on a street in Montreal.

When Chevillon and his fellow MED members hassled E & J into changing the wheel lock, the pins that held the swing away footrests began to fail. I'd be crossing a street and the footrest would suddenly swing out to the side, making me lose my balance and surprising any passerby that happened to be hit by it. The footrest pin problem was quickly replaced by the breakage of foot plates which was replaced by bad bearing which was replaced by — OK, keeping your chair usable was a challenge.

I was glad to go to work for the MED group. I knew they tended to drive E & J crazy, but a MED dealer could be a crip's best ally. But, I soon learned that finding out who and what MED was would involve a lot of research on my part. Chuck Chevillon explained that MED was a pretty tightly held secret. The members didn't want their competition to know what MED was up to — sometimes, even all of MED members didn't know.

Chuck was equally definitive about my job description, which was spelled out as "do what you have to do to make a catalog." What I had to do a lot of the time, it turned out, was to answer customer questions when all AAMED staff was tied up, learn what it took to rent a commode, find out how to get a specific wheelchair into Chicago from California in less than four months and try to identify every product that could possibly be used by a person with a disability. Chuck pointed out that this last task couldn't be limited to the United States or even the North American continent. It was good training. I learned the medical equipment sales and service business from all angles. Thanks to the fact that my MED office was in the AAMED building, I once even learned how to survive a strike against a medical equipment company by the Teamsters.

Getting to know the members of MED took a little more effort. I got to know Bob Kruse, AAMED's majority owner immediately. Bob had several outstanding characteristics. If it were 20° below zero in Chicago, Bob would give you his coat and the proverbial shirt off his back. Another of Bob's characteristics was his full-speed-ahead, zealous approach to life. He'd started AAMED out of his home, delivering oxygen to customers while his wife, Jimmi, answered phones, kept the books and took care of the five kids. Bob considered all of life to be a poker game. He'd take bets on whether the sun would come up in the morning. I learned not to eat breakfast at the same table with Bob in Las Vegas when he continued with his game of Keno by placing the card on top of my french toast. He won more than he lost.

He drove a car with the same wild abandon as he played games of chance. Other than the time he took part of the side out of the AAMED building with a delivery truck — or the time he launched his nephew's pick-up truck into Lake Michigan right behind Bob's sailboat — he was as lucky in driving as he was in playing cards.

Chuck, the more sedate of the two men, insisted on worrying about such things as whether the delivery trucks were on time, if the inventory levels were adequate or whether Abbey had stolen a sale from him that week. His first love, though, was to take a wheelchair and totally rebuild it until it did everything possible to make life easier for its user. To Chuck, the perfect way to spend Easter Sunday was to cut plywood and foam rubber and construct a seat in a chair that would make it possible for a little girl, whose condition caused extreme pain, to be mobile in a wheelchair. In his spare time, in addition to causing E & J to put him on their "the person we least like to have call the factory" list, Chuck played lawyer and wrote the by-laws for MED.

I'd only been with MED a few months when I met the rest of the cast of characters. Tom Dowd, from Buffalo, NY, and his brother, Jim, who had stores in Pittsburgh and Fort Lauderdale, FL, were pretty normal guys. Frank Jones was known for his fastidious nature. Not only was his store in Indianapolis, IN clean and shiny, with not a piece of paper out of place, he arrived at meetings with his white gloves so he could check that the local MED store had no hidden dirt in out-of-the-way places. Marty Frank had a perpetual tan and wiry, athletic build, matching his lifestyle in Los Angeles. Roy Jampsa, who owned Redi-Care, the Minneapolis-St. Paul-based stores brought into MED by Dewey Kuhn, had the typical Finnish sense of humor — barely noticeable — but a warm personality.

All of these guys were noticeably more intelligent and funnier than any group of men I'd met so far. The remainder of the group appeared to have been created by very clever screenwriters.

Nagle Bridwell, from Philadelphia, stood about 6'5" and,

as the others pointed out, filled any doorway he chose to stand in. Some people talk about helping others and putting their needs first. Nagle never mentioned it. He just did it. He frequently gave a person with a disability their first chance at high-level employment, then trained them to go on to even better things.

Lewie Lanham Bates, Jr., from Greenville, SC, was almost as tall as Nagle. After you got to know Lewie, you wondered how the confederacy had managed to lose the Civil War. Lewie talked slow — in fact, he claimed, he had to record the rest of us at 78 rpm and play us back at 33 1/3 rpm to understand what was going on. Lewie had no problems getting a job after graduating with a degree in engineering from Clemson University, but a week on the job in a northern city convinced him that he didn't particularly care to live by Yankee rules. Rebel rules, as practiced by Lewie, arbitrated a dispute with a truck freighting company by Lewie convincing the truck driver to back his rig into Lewie's warehouse and go get a soft drink. Lewie locked the warehouse and held the truck ransom until the freight company paid him the costs of shipping damages they owed him.

Don Redman, with stores in Phoenix and Tucson, was a clown. We never were able to go back to a Chicago restaurant after Redman took his serving of roast goose to the manager and told him to give the bird a drink of water and let it sleep overnight — it was so undercooked that it probably hadn't suffered any harm. Don's partner in the comedy skits that we called MED meetings was tall, droll Bud Gage, who had stores in Santa Rosa and Vallejo, CA. Bud once tried to convince Don, who never saw snow in Arizona, that the yellow spots in the snow along the sidewalks of Chicago was maple syrup and, therefore, edible.

Maybe it was because these men faced constant adversity in their businesses or maybe it was because the people they loved best to work with all had severe disabilities or maybe they had all been born jokers, for whatever reason, they carried on with the high spirits of a bunch of boys at Boy Scout camp. They had the perfect ringmaster/master-of-ceremonies/general trouble-stirrer in Ken Sandler, of Des Moines, IA.

Ken's sense of humor was so well-honed that we included a dinner at each MED meeting at which Ken would MC a trans-corporation roast, leaving no one undone. He would report which MED member now owned Don's stores after Don lost them in a poker game. He related Bob Kruse's latest adventures in clearing three lanes of the expressway within one mile with his driving style. He commiserated with Marty about how his business interfered with Marty's progress at becoming a tennis pro. He made verbal models of creations he claimed Chuck wished he had manufactured.

After he'd run through the MED members, he took on the manufacturers. When E & J was under investigation by the Department of Justice on charges of monopoly, unfair business practices and a bushel of other citations, Ken walked over to an E& J vice president with a sugar bowl from the restaurant table in his hand. "Would you mind speaking into the sugar bowl?" he asked the startled VP. "The justice department boys in the kitchen say they can't quite pick up everything you're saying."

Then there was the man we all lovingly called "Goddamnit!" His legal name was Dick DeVoe, who, with his partner, Ed Nelson, owned the MED store in Denver, Co. Dick sat in meetings and listened to the others until his feelings were evidently getting pretty pent-up — which is probably why his statement always began, "Goddamnit, Chuck — or whoever." When he called me on the phone, the first thing my secretary heard was, "Goddamnit! Where's Jan?" Dick was number two on E & J's list of "people we hate most to have call the factory." He once hired an E & J employee to come work at his store by calling late at night and having the night watchman put a "Job Available" posting on the factory bulletin board.

Dick could have posed as a model for the symbol of the 19th century rough-shod citizen of the wild west. He'd begun working in railroading, operating telegraphs to keep the trains on schedule — and out of impending collisions. He was working as a bill collector in Denver when one of the debtors he was pursuing stopped the pursuit by putting a bullet in Dick's spinal cord. He'd been one of Dr. Bob Jackson's favorite patients at Craig Rehabilitation Hospital — to the point that Jackson backed Dick financially when Dick decided to open his store, Wheelchairs, Inc.

He and Ed Nelson opened the store because, as Dick put it, "Goddamnit! A person ought to get everything he needs in a wheelchair. Somebody should go to bat for these fellas and gals." Dick went to bat. Did the patient need a custom manufactured wheelchair? Dick would get it out of the E & J plant in LA in 48 hours. Was the patient being given the run-around by social services? Dick would personally explain what services the patient was going to get — and he'd give the social worker all the details — the patient's name, cause of disability, former occupation, details of the house he lived in and the name and breed of the patient's dog. Dick was the only one of the MED men I was half afraid of — and I certainly jumped when he had a request.

This "damn the torpedoes — full speed ahead" style of management among the MED members made life a lot better for many people with disabilities. Once, a manufacturer had come up with a new design for a toilet seat that allowed the paralyzed person access to what needed to be reached and also aided in preventing pressure sores, which often had their start from a person sitting on the toilet too long. The problem was, the manufacturer needed an order for 200 of the seats before he could buy the components he needed to manufacture them.

Each MED member ordered a few. Chuck counted the order. It was still over 100 seats short. Chuck strode to the door of AAMED, where we were meeting, locked it and announced that no one would leave until all the seats were ordered. He went around the table a couple of times. Each man reluctantly added a few more models of a product he hadn't seen and didn't know would work to his inventory. Finally, Marty, tears rolling down his cheeks, took the last of the lot. We always wondered whether this episode was one of Marty's frequent collapses into hysterical laughter at his fellow MED members or whether it was because Marty, who was also notoriously frugal, was broken up at having to spend the money.

Chuck thought this means of helping a manufacturer introduce a new product was so effective that, over the years, he repeated it many times. This explains how the Graebe brothers were able to finance a wheelchair cushion that was so effective that it changed the lives of many, including Dick

DeVoe. The Roho cushion used a series of rubber balloons to support the weight of a person's body evenly across the buttocks and thighs. By reducing pressure on the bony parts of the buttocks, Roho frequently allowed people, who, like Dick, were prone to developing pressure sores, to stay in their wheelchairs and work longer hours without experiencing skin break down. Lewie referred to the wonder product as "a great big bowl of rubber prunes."

The MED "voluntary purchasing program" also explained why therapists and doctors always made sure to visit the MED booth at professional meetings. We had the new products first. The purchasing program also explains why, to this day, there are dozens of products in warehouses of MED and former MED stores, the merits of which were only perceived by MED. Actually, there were no such unwanted products in Ken Sandler's warehouse. He always convinced companies wanting to join MED that part of the membership requirement was to buy a selection of unsaleable products from him. After all, he was a corporate officer, wasn't he? Lewie went Ken one better. He offered to send the prospective member a selection of unwanted products — by taxi.

With the same enthusiasm — and naivete — that led MED to leap into introduction of unknown products, we dove into challenging the national catalog companies. It drove the guys crazy that "their therapists" ordered products using numbers the therapists had seen in national catalogs published by such companies as J. A. Preston and G. E. Miller. It made the guys even more frustrated when those therapists mailed an order to a catalog for a product that the MED member could supply from his warehouse.

It took a while to convince the lads that Preston had spent

years of work by a large staff and many, many dollars to develop a catalog of several hundred pages. We had one staff member and $250 per month per MED company. The guys became very supportive of a 48-page catalog on private label wheelchairs when presented with the estimate for a multi-100-page catalog. With Chuck becoming the official product photographer and me, the art director/copy writer/production manager, we soon had a catalog on the street that really made the competition wonder who MED was and what they were doing.

The private label wheelchairs were more than a marketing trick. The regular wheelchairs at that time would take about six months of hard use before back upholstery had to be replaced. A short time later, the wheels had to be replaced. MED had real leather capping sewn on the top of the back upholstery and offered three styles of heavy-duty wheels as a no-cost option. To make it easier for therapists to order, we developed our own product numbering system and gave them a supply of order forms with the numbering system diagrammed for quicker prescription. E & J supported these private label chairs enthusiastically — especially after Chuck and Nagle pointed out that some of the emerging, competitive wheelchair manufacturers were offering more than E & J.

Giving their customers better mobility wasn't the only concern of the MED men. They often first met their customer in a hospital or rehab center, but they continued to work with people with disabilities as they went home and back out into the world. Doing everyday tasks was frequently a challenge to people whose use of legs or arms or hands was limited. Small devices could bring back total independence. For example, how do you move safely from your wheelchair into your car if you can't stand up and your arms aren't strong enough to lift your body from the chair to the car?

There were a number of products on the market for what the therapists called Activities of Daily Living — ADL— but there weren't enough for MED. The guys agreed that such products needed to be better designed, available in more variety to suit the highly individualized needs of people with disabilities and more widely marketed.

It seemed like a good idea at the time for me to track down Gibb Fink, the intrepid boy inventor of anything anyone could possibly need. Chuck Chevillon and Gibb hit it off immediately and MED soon had literally hundreds of products that did things like hold a hand of cards if your hand wasn't strong enough. If you wanted to fix dinner, MED had a range of cutting boards and other devices to allow preparing food using only one hand.

Transfer boards got a little out of hand. We had transfer boards that hooked onto a wheelchair to keep the wheelchair in place while the person slid into his or her car. Some of our transfer boards folded so they could be carried on the wheelchair. Some were extra short, some extra long. Some were for use in the bathroom. Some were better for getting into bed. When we approached an even dozen types of transfer boards, the MED guys and I steered Chuck and Gibb on to other things. They responded by attempting to break a world record in devices that extended the reach of people in wheelchairs or with arm limitations. We had reachers to lift clothes off closet poles, reachers to pick books up off the floor, reachers to hold toilet paper and allow a person total privacy in the bathroom. I think we had a reacher to reach the other reachers.

MED became so well known for ADL items that we were asked to import products from England, Norway and Sweden. This brought us to the attention of other foreign manufacturers. Sweden, particularly, was far ahead of the USA in providing special products for people with disabilities. We soon found that we had become the USA office and caretaker of a wild Swedish inventor, Olle Blomqvist. Suddenly, we were in the therapy table and clinical equipment market. Olle liked us so much that he regularly came to the U.S. and tried to convince us that international trade was kind of like the Bible parable of the Good Samaritan. If you took on a foreign manufacturer's line, you were obligated to feed, house, provide transportation and otherwise care for him. Olle had himself some really great vacations in the U.S. When he got to our respective locations, he related highly imaginative explanations of why he had no money with him. On one trip to Las Vegas, Olle was robbed of his wallet 12 times. Unfortunately, his visa papers were in those wallets, so he couldn't go to the police. No problem. His friends in MED would loan him the money.

chapter 20

Products from the skunk works

In the mid-80's, books by management experts would coin the term "skunk works" for any product development done in an unorthodox manner. When Chuck was approached by a civic group from one of Chicago's western suburbs, who wanted to give more independence to a young woman who was living in a nursing home, MED came up with the mother of all skunk works. When Chuck met the woman, Margaret Pfrommer, a life-long bond was formed. Polio had left Margaret paralyzed to the extent that the only motion she could manage was moving her head from side to side a bit. She "frog breathed" by forcing air into her lungs with her tongue against the roof of her mouth.

"We can make it possible for Margaret to be out of bed and drive a power wheelchair," Chuck reported to his fellow MED members. It sounded reasonable to them. Nagle had happened on a crude, electro-mechanical device that operated four switches by sipping and puffing on a tube. One was shipped into Chicago immediately and Chuck turned engineer to figure out how this device could operate the four switches that controlled a power wheelchair.

If a person had been confined to bed as long as Margaret had, sitting in a chair in one position was going to cause fatigue — if not pressure sores. Bud Gage's staff reasoned that if the actuator used on wheelchair lifts for vans could be positioned properly, it could be used to raise and lower the back and leg rests of a reclining wheelchair. Dick DeVoe pointed out that the person's arms might fall off the armrests of the chair when their body changed position. DeVoe was also worried about damage to the shoulders if the hands and arms didn't move as the back of the chair reclined. Dick went into his shop and came out with an armrest for the wheelchair that cradled the person's arms and moved as the wheelchair back reclined.

Parts for Margaret's chair were flying in and out of Chicago from both coasts and the Rocky Mountains. The resulting wheelchair was like none ever seen before, but it worked. It needed a lot of care and tinkering, but it worked. Then it turned out that the guy, Nagle had come up with, who had made the sip and puff device was being sued by his former employer for stealing the idea. We didn't care about either side of the law suit. We wanted to make more of these marvelous machines. We did as we always did. We took a different route.

A friend of mine who ran education and training at RIC (Rehabilitation Institute of Chicago) told us to talk to the head of rehabilitation engineering for Northwestern University. This guy, my friend told me, was brilliant and a little crazy—sounded like he'd be the perfect match for MED.

Had we known Dudley Childress' international reputation

for brilliance in such areas as human joint replacement, bionics, and myoelectrics, we probably would have been too over-awed to approach him. We thought the technology that let you control four switches by the pressure of a puff of air moving an aluminum diaphragm a specific distance to complete an electrical contact was pretty exotic. Dudley thought capturing the electrical signals from the human brain and finding a way to direct them to move an artificial hand was elementary. He'd seen Margaret Pfrommer's chair. In fact, he'd arranged for Margaret to work part-time as the receptionist at the Northwestern University Rehabilitation Engineering Program which he headed. We could do much better than the system MED had toggled together, he assured Chuck and me. Just let him and his staff play with the idea a little.

Dudley and his staff of engineers were more at home designing printed circuit boards for electronics than they were with mowing their lawns. They also spent their time reading reports on electronic components. To them, a 15-page article filled with mathematical formulas, equations and small print was more exciting than an issue of *Playboy*. Within a short time, they'd found components from aircraft, telecommunications and other industries that could be stuck to a PCB — printed circuit board — to make a power wheelchair respond to sip and puff or a slight movement by a person's tongue just as well as the chair responded to the traditional joystick.

But, Margaret wanted the chair to handle better than it did with the joystick and she was an equal member of the MED and Northwestern team that broke the traditional rules of developing wheelchairs. True, Mr. Everest had told Mr. Jennings that he wanted his wheelchair to fold — back in the

1920's or 30's — but after that, wheelchairs were designed by people who weren't disabled. Sometimes, these designers hadn't ever met someone with a disability. Margaret, however, knew what worked for her — and she didn't consider the fact that she was totally paralyzed to be any reason not to coerce the Northwestern engineers into designing a system that made her able to be as functional as the next person.

Margaret found the abrupt start of the chair — 0 to 2 mph instantly — sometimes caused the sip and puff tube to be jerked out of her mouth. The instant stop of the chair when she sipped on the tube often threw her forward in the chair. The Northwestern engineers put a new chip on the PCB that made acceleration and deceleration adjustable. Margaret liked the idea of being able to move from a sitting to reclining position with the powered MED-I-Cliner that controlled the back and leg rests of her chair. Suddenly sitting straight up gave her the body language she wanted to emphasize her soft-spoken commands to the engineers. Gibb Fink thought he'd like to play with the MED-I-Cliner and make some improvements.

Dudley and his chief engineer on the project, John Strysik, liked safety. If the driver of the chair should lose control of the sip and puff tube, she must be able to stop the chair. They invented safety switches that needed only a slight turn of the head to activate. For a while, it seemed like the engineers were developing an average of one new component per week for the system. This project wasn't funded under any of the grants Northwestern had won, but it was more fun. They had instant feedback on their work from Margaret.

The MED guys went wild over their new toy. They'd always hated going into rehab clinics and having to tell people paralyzed from the neck down that their only option was to be pushed around by an attendant. Now, as one of the men put it, they could at least make it possible for a totally paralyzed person to leave the room on his own if he didn't like the other people in the room. It's probably better that we didn't know the meaning of the word "prototype" because the MED guys knew people all over the country that could use the new wheelchair system and they couldn't wait to get one to those people.

Nagle, Lewie, Marty and Dick ordered a bunch of what we now called the MED Quad Wheelchair. Politically correct hadn't arrived yet. People paralyzed from the neck down were still called quads because quadriplegic was too long to say and the people who needed the chair didn't care what we called them — just let them have one of the things so they could get on with their life. We liked our product so much that I threw together some advertisements and we bought space in *ACCENT on Living* — which was rather daring since we didn't have enough products to fill the requests that came in without advertising.

In later years, I learned the process for developing and introducing a product, which involved things like engineering prototypes, manufacturing prototypes, field testing, tooling for manufacturing, product instructions and a lot of other details. We were too excited by the reaction from our customers at being able to gain a measure of independence to bother with all those administrative details.

Dudley gently broke the news to us that development of the Quad System wasn't exactly what his department was being funded to do, but that was OK. Becoming a manufacturing source of the systems was probably going to stretch the limits of Northwestern's extremely patient administration. We looked around for a company that could manufacture the electronic circuit boards and switches. Chuck's and my offices became the ordering assembly, packing and shipping departments. The guys at the MED stores became used to me calling to see if I'd accidently used the layout sheets for the next catalog as packing material.

Supervising manufacturing was challenging. Chuck questioned why John Strysik and I were roaming around Chicago's suburbs looking for companies that manufactured circuit boards for copy machines, television sets — anything that demanded a high standard of reliability. Learning about different areas has always been my hobby. From John, I learned that the solder on PCB's should be good enough to get the current from one end of the board to the other consistently. John also taught me to install one of two switch options on the board because it saved some money if all the boards were basic. Besides, it was only a matter of a few bolts a little bigger than darning needles and what else did I have to do on Saturday afternoons?

What MED lacked in knowledge of the correct procedures for product introduction, they made up with enthusiasm and the determination to get their customers "on the road". By coincidence, MED developed a field testing process that most manufacturers of products for the disabled would kill for. Nagle served Moss and Magee rehab hospitals in Philadelphia. Chester Black had joined MED and his PDC, Inc. in Boston served Tufts and two other top spinal cord injury centers. Lewie had a rehab center in Greenville and drove to Atlanta to cover two or three more each week.

Marty served a number of the many rehab centers in the LA area. Dick worked in Craig daily and had the challenge of people from all over the nation, who had been flown to Craig because of the complexity of their injuries. Chuck had three Chicago rehab centers — and would always disassemble a couple of power chairs and load them in the trunk of his Caddy to fit patients in Illinois, Indiana, Michigan and Wisconsin.

Product performance reviews were informal. There wasn't time to write down comments because product review usually was when the phone rang and one of the MED guys would demand an instant fix. Dick DeVoe was the most demanding. A conversation with Dick often went as follows:

"Goddamnit, Jan! You've got to get a couple of new circuit boards and safety switches on the plane this afternoon! Calvin's quad chair is down. You know Calvin — he's the one who got his neck stepped on by a bull when he was a rodeo rider and he and his wife bought this ranch up in Montana and they raise rodeo stock — well, he has to keep going!"

"Dick, Calvin weighs 300 pounds — and he insists on running the chair up and down grassy hills," I would reply. "The motors and electronics can't take that. Besides, last week you told me a cow sat on Calvin's chair..."

"It was a steer, goddamnit! Besides, if we're going to sell this stuff, it has to work. Calvin's got to do what he wants to..."

Another source of good feedback on what the chairs were doing in the field was Lewie's shop manager, Ol' Earl. Ol' Earl was more laid back than Dick.

"Ya'll got my boards fixed?" Earl began one conversation.

"Oh, I put a bigger fuse in Mr. Jones' chair. It keeps blowing out. I know ya'll said that he should stop giving his kids rides — he lets them sit on his chest when the MED-I-Cliner goes up and down..."

The standard answer was, "Earl, you know the MED-I-Cliner motor wasn't designed to be an amusement ride. If you fuse the chair any higher, Mr. Jones is going to go up in a puff of smoke..."

"Well, his young 'uns are just so happy to have Daddy home from the hospital, I hate to ruin their fun. Is Andy's boards fixed yet?"

"They'll be on their way tomorrow. Would you like to explain why they were covered with mud and sand? John swears he found a couple of tadpoles on those boards."

"Well," Earl would reply, "Ya'll know how much Andy likes to fish — me and Mr. Bates fixed him up a fishin' rig that he can reel in with a sip and puff switch. Seems Andy hooked a pretty big one and he got so excited that he puffed on the wrong tube and the chair kind of took off the end of the pier — water weren't very deep there so's it weren't real serious..."

The customer, claimed the MED guys, was always right. After all, the quad system was supposed to let a person do what he or she wanted to do, wasn't it? We didn't worry about product liability. Our customers didn't want to sue — they wanted to fish, or raise rodeo stock or amuse the kids. Some of them said that they were glad to test the quad systems. It might mean more people with severe disabilities could have the opportunity for more freedom.

Not many companies had MED's attitude of "work with the customer and take care of what they want to do — and worry about getting sued when and if it happens". We were doing something American business can't afford to do in enlisting our customers as part of the team to get this product going. Maybe it's just as well that this practice never became widespread. It could have put thousands of lawyers out of business.

Over twenty years later, some legislators are talking about changing the tort laws so that people in need of new medical procedures can participate in trials without exposing suppliers to liability suits. If the Quad System project had waited for such an enlightened stance, Margaret Pfrommer would never have been able to travel extensively and lecture on opportunities for people with severe disabilities. She wouldn't have had the chance to start some of the support services she started either. The law would have protected her right to spending her life in a nursing home.

Customers took to the Quad System much quicker than many doctors we ran into. The doctors at Craig and RIC and the other facilities served by MED welcomed the unit. One doctor in Boston thought the benefits of the MED Quad System were so great that he kept six complete systems on hand at all times. As soon as one of his patients with a spinal cord injury in the cervical area was in stable medical condition, Dr. Freed got them up and proved to them that they would have some independence. He felt it helped them be more willing to work at getting out of the hospital.

Reception of the MED Quad System by doctors we met at the exhibits held in conjunction with medical meetings was frequently less enthusiastic. There was one memorable moment at one show when a doctor asked me what the tray mounted across the bottom frame of the wheelchair was for.

I explained that our dealers used the tray to carry a portable respirator onboard the chair so that a person with spinal cord damage above the third cervical vertebra could be independent despite the fact they could not breathe independently. The doctor explained to me — in a combination of patience and condescension — that people always died from injuries so high in their spinal column. The MED guys manning the booth with me suppressed their delight as one of the doctors from RIC, who happened to be standing by, looked at the first doctor and said, "My God! This means I have got to go back to Chicago and tell six of my patients they're really dead and don't know it!"

Each trade exhibit at which we showed the MED Quad System was a new adventure. We may have initiated the practice, still used by manufacturers in the medical equipment trade, of introducing a product that was going to be on the market soon. In reality, we put the first model together in our booth at the show.

At least we found out that switches activated by the moisture in a person's breath weren't a good idea in humid climates. At a show in Houston, the MED-I-Cliner caused the wheelchair to recline and sit up in frantic repetition every time the truck doors of the exhibit hall were opened, letting in a blast of Houston's 98% water atmosphere. Another time, we forgot to tune transmitters on two of the chairs in our booth to different frequencies. The hapless MED guy demonstrating one chair could only do what the guy in the other chair happened to be doing at the moment.

Meanwhile, back in Chicago, Margaret, having tired of make shift environmental controls, had spurred the engineers off on the search for a better way to remotely control lights, appliances and other things that operated on electricity. The Micro-Dec was born. Micro-Dec was a plastic box about the size of a book with an LED (light emitting diode) display of numbers representing 16 channels. Puffing on the tube that also drove a Quad Chair, caused the unit to cycle through the numbers. Each number represented a specific function — turn on the desk lamp, for example. When the user reached the number he or she wanted, a puff would activate the function. Micro-Dec also could be used to record a telephone number, complete with area code, then dial the telephone to complete the call.

Demands for the MED wheelchair and environmental control systems grew. Our service, repair and training demands grew in an exponential fashion. MED finally broke down and let me hire a technician to assemble components, repair and troubleshoot the units. We had to move out of AAMED and use most of our new office space as a production and repair shop.

The MED group, which by now had 45 to 50 stores — depending on how many Nagle had opened that month — found that introducing new products was the most satisfying thing they'd ever done in their businesses. Never mind that it wasn't profitable, they argued. They probably made it up in new customers, who bought other items after coming to a MED company for the specialty items. Besides, they told each other at meetings, you really can't put a dollar figure on seeing somebody able to do something they thought they'd never be able to do again.

While the federally-funded departments that addressed disability were developing elaborate programs to design and distribute new products for people with disabilities, the most exciting products were the result of skunk works, common sense — which Lewie termed "mule technology" — and blind optimism. MED had ventured into the field of alternative and augmentative communications with products from Sweden. Our products were made obsolete by devices made by a young engineer named Larry Weiss, from Portland, Oregon. Larry's never admitted to me that he probably mortgaged his house or in some other fashion raised the capital without federal grants to start developing systems that allowed people who couldn't talk to express themselves by activating lighted squares on a communications board. His switch options could be used by pounding on a paddle, sipping and puffing or using the uncontrolled gross movements often found in people with cerebral palsy.

chapter 21

While the feds fund, the people do

S ome of the federal grant money for developing products
for people with disabilities was well used. For example,
research by Gregg Vanderheiden at the University of Wisconsin, revealed that hundreds — perhaps thousands — of
people with cerebral palsy had been wrongly diagnosed as
retarded. The majority were far from retarded. They were instead unable to make others know their thoughts because
they could not speak intelligibly. Gregg and his staff designed some prototypes of advanced communications devices.

It was Barry Romich, however, who risked losing his
thriving electronic manufacturing business by turning to designing, building and training people to use electronic communications devices on a widespread basis. Barry's units
could be programmed by the person who used them to provide the desired vocabulary.

It was always fun working with Barry when he made it
possible for some of his customers to demonstrate their elec-

tronic speech capabilities. Some of those customers had been denied speech until in their teens and they were tired of being treated like vegetables by people who didn't know them. Some of the vocabularies they programmed could have had their origin in the navy. At one meeting, one of Barry's clients took all he could of a speech by a woman, who was proclaiming her dedication to helping these poor unfortunate folks with disabilities. His electronically amplified comment on her speech dealt with a by-product of raising cattle.

MED soon attracted the attention of other rehabilitation engineers who were frustrated by not being able to get their products to the people who needed them most. At meetings, these engineers noticed that Dudley's work had spread rapidly and was even being copied by major companies. Could their products take the same route?

Doug Hobson, a gentle, bearded giant of a man, knew that children with cerebral palsy did not have to grow up to have skeletal deformities that cut their pain-ridden lives short. He and his wife, Elaine Trefler, had studied methods of supporting the bodies of such children in wheelchairs so that deformities might be avoided. Elaine also believed she saw such children becoming more functional, alert and able to learn if they were supported in a manner that made them use some of their muscles. This differed from the accepted practice of placing the child in a slightly reclined position and putting padding around their bodies to keep them still. Elaine sometimes remarked that she thought she would become pretty bored if her view of the world all day was the ceiling of the room — as it was for children strapped into semireclined wheelchairs.

Doug and Elaine and their staff at the University of Tennessee at Memphis had designed a number of seating and positioning products. While colleagues in rehabilitation engineering tended to believe that each child's seat had to be individually designed and fabricated, Doug believed that a basic seating system could be made in mass-produced modular units that would meet the needs of a significant percentage of children with cerebral palsy. This would decrease the cost of seating a child properly and make it possible for many more children to benefit. Now, they needed someone to commercialize the designs. MED decided it was a good idea to try.

Each MED company threw some money in the pot to pay for manufacturing, stocking and shipping the products. They each agreed to send members of their staffs to Memphis to be trained by Doug and Elaine and their staff to fit the systems. We were soon on our way.

Actually, I was on my way to Memphis to work with Red Lee, our MED member there to get manufacturing under way. Red was what's known as a good ol' boy. He didn't talk much Yankee, but he got to the point quickly.

"Ya'll ready to go out in the sticks?" he asked as he picked me up at the Memphis airport. "The guy that makes the plastic parts is out near Dyersburg — the guy that makes the metal parts ain't rightly near any place."

We wandered through the Tennessee hills and forests for quite a while before we saw the sign, "Dyersburg — Mule Capitol of the World."

"Where's the town?" I asked Red.

"Yer lookin' at it — that there's the mayor's house — ya can tell because it's got a new washing machine on the front porch — curtains, too..."

We pulled up in front of a house that didn't have any washing machine on the front porch. It turned out to be the town restaurant, cocktail lounge, gas and service station. Red's reasoning was practical. Not only could we get some Tennessee barbeque for lunch, we could meet the owner of the plastics production plant there and he could take us back to the plant. Red wasn't afraid of getting lost. He just wanted one of the local citizens along when we went deeper into the hills. You never know, Red pointed out, when city folks like us might get mistaken for a "revenuer" and be shot at by the local citizens.

Red and I spent most of our time that hot, humid summer trekking around the woods and hills in that part of Tennessee to get molds made and metal frames manufactured. Many times, work had to be scheduled around more important things — like the fish biting real good.

At the same time, MED staff members were learning to fit the system — which Doug gave the very imaginative name of MPI for molded plastic inserts — for specific children. Although Elaine and Susan Johnson Taylor and Doug were the nominal instructors for the courses, the kids with whom we worked were the real instructors. As part of the team put together at the University of Tennessee, children and young adults with cerebral palsy provided the input that made the system successful.

One young girl who taught all of us what could be achieved when a person has the appropriate technology to work with was Lainie. Lainie had been thought by many medical professionals to be profoundly retarded. Her physical capability was certainly limited by athetoid movements

— uncontrolled jerking of the arms, legs and trunk. Lainie's movements were so strong and uncontrolled that her arms had to be totally restrained to enable her to use her neck and head. With her head and neck, Lainie could operate a communications device, drive her wheelchair and, while she was at it, totally charm anyone she encountered. In later years, she went on to college and used her eloquence and perception to assist other people with disabilities.

Many products that would help a person with a disability lead an active life aren't available to the people who need them for any number of reasons. The market for such products is small and scattered so it isn't practical for a large company to spend the large amounts of money necessary to introduce the product. Small companies and inventors frequently run out of funds before their product reaches the people who need it. A perverse situation exists with these products. The market isn't large because people don't know there is a product that could help them. People with disabilities can't create a demand or, therefore, a market if they don't learn of the product. To further block the paths of people with disabilities in their quest to find products that would make their lives better, many such products are purchased for people with disabilities by private and government funding agencies. These agencies won't buy the products until they are proven to be effective. The products can't be proven to be effective until they're purchased and used.

The apparent reality of trying to use available technology — in this case, simple plastic thermoform molding to help a kid sit in a more stable position and use his or her body — is that it can't be done through accepted methods. The people at the University of Tennessee certainly couldn't afford to finance widespread field tests — or place ads in family magazines — or advertise on TV. It was a good thing that Doug Hobson and Elaine Trefler didn't understand the basic principles of product introduction and marketing. Thousands of children with cerebral palsy would never have benefited from seating and positioning products developed at U of T.

Fortunately, there were others who ignored the rules and proven theories about how products are developed and introduced. In addition to MED, a young prosthetist and orthotist believed that he could make a difference in the lives of children and adults whose disabilities could restrict sitting and using their hands.

Michael Silverman could have remained comfortable in the prosthetics/orthotics business built by his father, Oscar, but instead chose to start from scratch and develop an entire company to make products including those developed at U of T available to all who needed them. U of T had some federal funding to start the designs. Oscar sold his profitable company to help Michael start the new company, Pin Dot.

Michael used the good old American way of business called knowing everything there is to know about the customer — not through marketing studies, but by talking and working with the customer. It also involved Michael traveling about 390 days a year — Michael being a very fast moving and efficient fellow. If a technique — like computer-aided design and manufacture (CAD/CAM) — worked for auto makers and machinery manufacturers, Michael reasoned, then it could be used to design proper body support for people with disabilities that resulted in potentially fatal deformities.

The product introduction methods used by the successful

people like Michael Silverman and Barry Romich might well have sent the more organized medical establishment into cardiac arrest. Both Michael and Barry are famous for on-the-spot aid. Parents of children with disabilities face a constant battle to find anything that will make their child's life better, but it's usually only through word-of-mouth from other parents that they learn of a product, like Barry's communications devices. In our very disorganized medical and health care system, it is frequently necessary for such parents to do whatever it takes.

I was never at a product exhibition where Barry was demonstrating equipment that I didn't see him quietly arrange for parents to bring their child to him. He would then find a quiet time to work with the child and determine what type of communications device the kid could use, often working for several hours to help the child become comfortable. Then, he'd provide the parents with every conceivable idea on how the product could be funded through the parents' insurance. If that failed, he usually found a "used" unit. Michael once paid for a team of experts in seating to travel across several states to correct a seating system which had been prescribed in a manner that actually endangered the child. The original prescribers had also overcharged the parents several thousand dollars.

This do-whatever-it-takes method of marketing is well illustrated by one of the sessions conducted by Chuck Chevillon when MED was first introducing the MPI.

We were showing equipment at a health fair in a shopping mall in a small, central Illinois town. The second day of the fair, a family came to our booth with a beautiful little girl who had cerebral palsy. A neighbor had seen the funny-looking wheelchair that helped kids sit up and brought the family in to see if we could help. They'd even taken up a collection in case little Susie — or whatever her name was — could be helped. "Oh, no!" I cautioned Chuck. "We'll probably be arrested for practicing without a license or something."

Undaunted, Chuck found a quiet spot in the mall, grabbed a selection of seats and backs and a wheelchair frame and trooped off with the family — complete with grandparents, aunts, uncles and a wide assortment of relatives. He picked up Susie, cuddling her and talking to her to help her relax. Then he placed her in the seating system and adjusted it to her.

Suzie had one position, it seemed — arms lying on the tray of her wheelchair and head buried in those arms. Chuck adjusted the angle of the seat and back, just as Elaine had taught him. After considerable holding of collective breaths, he finally found the angle that let Susie get control of her head and neck. When Chuck put his shiny, jiggly bunch of keys on the wheelchair tray, Susie slowly smiled and reached out to grasp the keys. The family thought it was a miracle. We knew it was an indication that more training and imagination is needed in working with and treating kids like Susie.

In the decade of the 1970's, working with MED provided an opportunity to see the beginning of a new attitude toward people with disabilities. Progress was being made. Attitudes were moving from cure for a disability being the only acceptable goal to making the most of the ability a person did have. While federal programs and health care administrations wrote ponderous studies on what might be possible, a lot of very individualistic people with very creative minds went ahead and contented themselves with just solving problems. Generally, they were too busy solving problems to write theories. Usually, these doers were looked down upon by health care professionals.

One of the most frequent criticisms we heard from therapists, doctors and funding agency personnel was that we charged for our services. "How can you charge $7,000 for a wheelchair?" a doctor would ask. Being the smart alecs we were, we replied, "Well, this chair allows the person to change positions — which might avoid a pressure sore that would cost $50,000 to treat medically — and be independent, so their family members can work to keep the whole family off welfare. By the way, doctor, I assume you do not receive payment for your services." We were careful to do that only to doctors that we knew weren't in the market for our services anyway.

As a person with a disability — and a taxpayer — the trap in which the health care and welfare system of the U.S. ensnared people with disabilities annoyed me. The policies for funding of services and equipment and those for support of people with disabilities were — and as of this writing, still are — archaic. Evidently, whoever is in charge of health and human services finds it easier to force disabled people and their families to be supported on public aid than to work with each case individually.

We at MED became involved in one typical illustration of these policies when we designed a MED Quad System for a farmer from southern Illinois. He had been left paralyzed from the neck down and unable to speak following an accident. When his insurance funding was exhausted, the state mandated that his family sell the farm and "spend down" their resources to meet the qualifications for state assistance. Doctors at the Rehabilitation Institute of Chicago were so irate that they challenged the decision and won a variance.

In the end, the family was allowed to keep their farm and the father spent his ten remaining years of life teaching his sons to run the farm. His chair, controlled by sip and puff, fit quite nicely in the front end loader of the farm tractor so he could go into the fields and check the crops. His communications device let him direct his sons' efforts. By spending a minimal amount to help get the family back in business, the state of Illinois probably saved well over $500,000 that would have been required to support the family on state assistance.

MED continued to carry on as the mavericks of the industry. We didn't know what couldn't be done, so we did it. The early MED members operated under the delusion that they were frontier gunslingers — or something similar. Traveling with Dick DeVoe and I taught them about accessibility. Getting Jan to the bathroom resulted in such adventures as one MED member whipping out his tool kit — which MED men never left home without — and instantly making a ladies room in a restaurant accessible. He just tore out one of the partitions. We always sent the guys with the thickest southern accents into the ladies rooms to clear the way. Ladies, subjected to their southern charm, were less likely to have them arrested.

We continued to travel across the country demonstrating our latest products at professional conferences and trade shows. Dick DeVoe and I began to notice that, toward the end of the decade of the 70's, we were no longer the only people using wheelchairs manning exhibits and developing products to let people with disabilities go about their business. The product area the government would later label "assistive technology" was coming of age.

People with disabilities no longer were passively accepting what nondisabled designers thought was good. Rather, the people who used the products were beginning to dictate design. A wheelchair is not a good substitute for legs that function, but, if a person is going to rely on a wheelchair, it should be the easiest to use. We began to see new ideas — and the erosion of the old attitude of "well, if you're crippled, you can't do much anyway — so what difference does it make if your wheelchair pushes like a lead sled?"

chapter 22

Disneyland on the Potomac

During the decade of the '70's, many people with disabilities had decided that life was to be lived to the fullest. Those people were already working at jobs, raising families and pursuing sports. A small industry had emerged to design and manufacture products that assisted with mobility, speech and everyday activities.

In the mid-1970's, the United States government made the startling discovery that there were people out there with disabilities who lived in the community — not in nursing homes. The government didn't know how many people like that were out there because the only disabled people they could count were those that did live in nursing homes or were supported by government programs such as social security.

It may have dawned on the legislators that there were enough people with disabilities, who wanted to be active in communities, to raise enough fuss that the Rehabilitation Act of 1973 was amended to include Public Law 90-480, PL

91-205, PL 95-125, PL 95-557, PL 94-142, PL 95-49, PL 95-561, PL 95-44, PL 95-524, and PL's 95-171, 95-216, 95-291, 95-600 and 96-265. The first nine of these amendments basically said that people with disabilities should be able to get into buildings built with their tax money even if those people used a wheelchair and that people with disabilities had a right to equal education and employment opportunities. The last five amendments dealt with social security and are still being interpreted.

The average citizen, who takes the time to think about how legislation is initiated, may suspect that a problem or issue that touches the lives of one of the legislators gets attention sooner than abstract things like the International Money Supply. This was the case when Representative Olin Teague, from Texas, began his quest to improve the lives of the handicapped.

Teague had one of his legs amputated as the result of complications from an injury suffered in the war. Like thousands of amputees before him, Teague soon found that, in many ways, prosthetic limbs hadn't been greatly improved since the days of the Civil War when any old oak tree was a good, basic artificial leg. Teague's leg was probably made of plastics and newer materials, but it was still a pain in the stump — and, evidently other portions of the good congressman's anatomy. Teague also hired an aide who had not one, but two prosthetic legs. They both found roaming the multi-miles halls of Capitol Hill a bother.

Teague got even grumpier about the whole situation when he discovered that some guy out in Michigan had invented a neat little three wheeled, battery-operated scooter that was the perfect thing for scooting to the House when it was time to vote, but the scooter didn't qualify as medical equipment and, therefore, was not reimbursed by either Medicare nor private insurance.

"If we can put a man on the moon," Teague argued, "why can't we use all this technology to make people walk?"

The topic seemed ideal for launching a congressional investigation. The United States House of Representatives Committee on Science and Technology Subcommittee on Technology and the Handicapped was formed. Since the acronym USHRCSTSTH was both cumbersome and non-pronounceable, everybody started calling it the Teague Committee. In addition to some congressmen and some senators — who were members of the United States Senate Committee on Science and Technology — a number of other people were included in the project under the title United States House of Representatives Committee on Science and Technology Subcommittee on Technology and the Handicapped Advisory Committee. These members represented the National Space and Aeronautics Administration (NASA), the Veterans Administration, the Rehabilitation Service Administration, the American Orthotics and Prosthetics Association and a few other Washington organizations.

After a bit of time, someone — probably Sherman Roodzant, Teague's doubly-amputated aide — had an idea. How about including some people with disabilities in this investigation? This group became the Advisory Panel to the Advisory Committee to the — read the above paragraph. To ensure impartiality of the participants — no one wanted the people who used wheelchairs to have more say-so than those who used white canes — representatives of various types of disabilities were selected.

Frank Bowe, who is deaf, had already made numerous waves in Washington with both his eloquently written and spoken arguments for equal opportunities for those with hearing impairment. Larry Scadden, who is blind, had also gained national recognition with his work promoting equal opportunities for people with sight impairment and in the area of technical aids for the blind. Lex Freiden, a dynamic Texan, had many accomplishments in the area of providing independent living opportunities for people with disabilities. Lex, who, like Frank and Larry, has had a long career of assuring new benefits for people with disabilities, is paralyzed from the neck down.

Jim Seybold, a paraplegic as a result of an injury in the Korean War and a leader in the Paralyzed Veterans of America organization, represented veterans. Evidently, the advisory panel to the advisory committee must have decided that women with disabilities should be represented because, shortly after the panel convened, Jim called me and asked me to join the group.

This was the beginning of my chance to learn how the nation's laws are made. I had missed the traditional annual trip to Washington, DC made by my high school classmates. I made up for that omission by traveling to Washington so often over the next two decades that I was personal friends with every United Airlines crew that flew that route.

The first thing that strikes a first-time visitor to Washington is the size of the federal buildings and how the city is laid out. Thanks to M'sieur L'Enfant, the spokes-of-a-wheel design, though beautiful, confuses the average visitor. It wasn't until 1987 that I could reliably find my way from Q

Street to I Street. The second thing that struck me was that our nation's capitol was accessible. Not only were there cutout curbs at many street corners and ramps on many buildings, I found that, by going into the street and waving my arm, a cab would stop for me. The driver would cheerfully get out and put my chair into the cab after I climbed into the front street.

This was a new experience. In Chicago, a person in a wheelchair catches a cab by having a hotel doorman threaten to ban the cabbie from ever making another pickup at that hotel. Then the passenger bribes the cabbie to load the wheelchair in the trunk — all in one piece if possible. Then the passenger is told that in order to ride in the front seat — necessary because the back door of cabs doesn't open far enough to slide into the back seat — the passenger will have to get a letter from the office of the mayor of Chicago allowing a variance to the city ordinance banning passengers' riding in the front seat of the cab unless the rear seat already has three people sitting on it. At the end of the ride, the passenger bribes the cabbie to get the chair out of the trunk and bring it to the front of the cab.

I liked the Washington way so much that I frequently took cabs to places I wasn't going — then took another one back.

The people in Washington were very friendly, too. In those days, I was too poor to afford a television set — which led to my being unable to recognize congressmen when I saw them in person. This in turn led to the nice man who held my chair as I was getting out of a cab and helping me up a curb having to introduce himself as Hubert Humphrey — from Minnesota, he added. I did better with Senator Paul Simon of Illinois. He always sent us voters a Christmas card with a picture of his family and their dog. I also learned to recognize Ted Kennedy. He would cross a busy hotel lobby to shake hands with someone in a wheelchair.

Excited from my day of exploring Washington and confident that I had something to offer to the advisory panel, I trundled off to one of the many federal buildings to attend the first meeting. It was a stroke of luck that I'd met Larry Scadden, who was staying at the same hotel were I was staying. If Larry hadn't escorted me, I'd have never found the meeting room.

These guys on the advisory committee and advisory panel were really very nice, cheerful fellows, I thought. They all smiled at me when I suggested that my contribution for the next meeting would be to compile a list of the agencies in the federal government that addressed problems of the handicapped — this was before politically correct took over and we were still allowed to use the word "handicapped." Actually, not all the guys just smiled. A retired naval admiral and the NASA representative were evidently very pleased with my suggestion. They couldn't stop laughing for a while.

By the time the next month's meeting was held, I'd tracked down 157 different agencies that dealt with some aspect of physical handicaps. Gently and patiently, the panel chairman explained to me that these agencies were not even in the same branches of government, let alone the same departments. Each agency had its own staff and budget and responsibilities — and they certainly didn't go around talking to each other and muddying the waters by crossing the lines. The responsibility of the committee, he reminded us, was to develop a new agency with the specific function of helping the handicapped by making technology available to them.

Never one to learn from a single experience, my next effort to contribute to the panel's work was to produce an outline of the factors that were inhibiting access to state-of-the-art technology by people with handicaps. I was pretty proud of that piece. It addressed the fact that identification of significant market masses was difficult, if not impossible, which resulted in lack of incentive for private industry to develop new products. I went on to discuss the cumbersome nature of a market in which a product was prescribed by someone other than the person who would use it and paid for by a funding source that had contact with neither the prescriber nor the end user. Furthermore, I continued, the cost of product liability insurance in any area that could vaguely be considered health care prohibited a manufacturer from taking risks with new products.

Two of my fellow panelists took me to lunch and explained that I just wasn't getting it. The purpose of the committee was to form an agency which could authorize studies to find out why people with disabilities couldn't get the technology they needed. We weren't there to form any conclusions. And, furthermore, did I think the NASA representative was there because he got in the wrong room? The space race had cooled and who was better prepared to develop technology for the handicapped than NASA.

After almost two years of meetings nearly every month, the advisory committee and panel drafted a hefty report for the sub-committee, which in turn drafted a larger report for the House of Representatives Committee on Science and Technology, which drafted a larger report for the Joint House and Senate Committee, which drafted a monstrous report for congress. It took UPS three days to deliver my copy of the report to my home — of course, UPS had a 25-pound per destination, per day, limit in those days.

Congress acted upon the recommendations by forming an agency in the Department of Health, Education and Welfare. This agency, the National Institute of Handicapped Research was charged with issuing grants to university and rehabilitation research facilities to study the problems of how to get technology to people with disabilities. When it became politically unacceptable to use the word "handicapped," the institute was renamed the National Institute for Disability and Rehabilitation Research. NIDRR was temporarily orphaned when HEW was split into Health and Human Services and the Department of Education, but finally found a home at DOE.

By this time, congressmen had realized that legislation to help people with disabilities ranked right up there in the minds of their constituencies with caring for widows and orphans. As a topic, it certainly was more popular with the constituents than saving the Mallard Duck.

Despite the Institute to Facilitate Access to Technology by People with Disabilities — NIDRR — congress still wasn't sure how well federal agencies were working for the average Joe Paraplegic, who just wanted to be able to get a couple of things that made it possible for him to get around town, earn a living and shoot pool when he wanted to. So, the Senate Committee on Labor and Human Resources requested that the Office of Technology Assessment — OTA — look into just what all of these departments, bureaus and agencies dedicated to helping the handicapped were accomplishing.

OTA responded that the committee had to recognize that studying technology for the handicapped was an "extremely broad and complex range of issues" and that the committee needed to authorize funding for a planning study to plan how to do the study. The committee did.

In 1982, the Office of Technology Assessment completed the planning study and was authorized more funding to do a study which reported on the factors which prevent access to technology by people with disabilities. They found that identification of market masses was difficult, technology was not selected by the people who wished to use it but prescribed by someone else and paid for by a funding source that had contact with neither the prescriber nor end user. The report finished off with the opinion that the high cost of product liability was prohibiting new product development by manufacturers. I could have told them that. Any manufacturer could have told them that — and they work cheaper than the government.

Of course, the government had more resources with which to conduct the study, right? After all, we pay taxes to support all those various departments — Commerce, Health and Human Services — and bureaus — like the U.S. Bureau of Census. Surely, the OTA could use records from those departments. Guess again. The Department of Commerce used to send me detailed reports when I was editing food magazines. At a glance, a person could find out how much cocoa, sugar, wheat or whatever the U.S. had used in any given period. How many cars were produced? The figures were there — right down to the specific model.

However, manufacturers of wheelchairs are not hooked into the same reporting system as manufacturers of other durable goods. What's more, although the wheelchair manufacturers, as publicly-held companies, must issue annual reports, they're not about to reveal their wheelchairs sales to the competition. The annual report just gives dollar amounts — you can try to guess at how much volume was in wheelchair sales.

Health and Human Services doesn't really know how many people in the U. S. use wheelchairs. Their survey is based on a relatively small number of people and extrapolated to the general population with the results expressed as "limited in mobility."

Although the U.S. Census Bureau changed its policy in the 1990's to try to capture some numbers on various disabilities, at the time of the OTA Report, the Census knew how many people used the bathroom in the homes surveyed, but had no idea how many people had to slide onto the toilet from a wheelchair. The Veterans Administration knew how many chairs they paid for each year, but didn't know how many veterans went out and bought a chair that they could use instead of being issued a "depot" chair from the VA.

The OTA interviewed dozens of people connected with the wheelchair industry. All of us marketing people guessed at how many wheelchairs our company sold in a year and how many our competitors sold. OTA took the results, did some statistical massaging and came up with numbers. OTA gave up on such things as aids for bathing, things to help people in their jobs and the rest of the technology products that make people with disabilities functional.

chapter 23

Disability on Capitol Hill

O TA reports have a specific purpose. They become the basis for a congressional hearing. The congressmen would hear testimony from people acquainted with disability and technology. This testimony would be used to determine if the information in the OTA study — which had been drawn from hundreds of articles by people dealing with technology and the handicapped and interviews with about 300 people with handicaps, was based on what people who published articles and people who used technology thought about the topic.

Most of us who were called upon to testify didn't spend much time in preparation. We dusted off the notes we'd used when the OTA had interviewed us or reviewed our articles for the study. Besides, by this time, we'd worked together for over ten years in meetings held on technology and the handicapped sponsored by the Veterans Administration, the Rehabilitation Service Administration, NIDRR and a number of other government agencies. Not only could we automatically give our own speeches that we'd been using for ten years — we could give each other's speeches.

After Barry Romich rescued me from the security guard at the door of the Senate Office Building — who'd never seen a hand-held hair dryer like the one in my suitcase and was convinced it was a lethal weapon — I remarked to Barry that we must be awfully early for the hearing. There were only two people at the tables reserved for the members of the congressional panel that was holding the hearing. Barry, much more sophisticated in the ways of Washington than I, broke the news to me. Congressmen and women didn't actually attend these hearings. They would have their aides scan *The Congressional Record* later if they needed any of the information.

The morning session was spent on testimony from people with disabilities telling how the system failed to work for them. One woman told of having to sue the city of New York to allow her to teach after she had earned her degree in education with funding from the federally sponsored vocational rehabilitation services administered by the state of New York. Another told of being able to hold a job and earn enough to feed and house himself. However, the power wheelchair repairs had strained his budget to the extent that he wasn't able to find $25,000 to replace the van voc rehab had funded in order for him to be able to work. Lacking any way to get to work, he'd had to quit his job and go back on public support.

Another man had found family members from whom to borrow the money for his law school education after his voc rehab counselor had determined he could not be a lawyer because he couldn't lift the law books. The man, paralyzed from the neck down, was currently the assistant attorney general of a large, midwestern state. There weren't any success stories. Evidently, any people with disabilities who were making a decent living in spite of the help of the government didn't choose to use their own money to come testify.

Some obscure reasoning on the part of the people choosing those who would testify determined that, because I worked for a commercial manufacturer of technology for the disabled, I was not disabled. I joined Barry and Jim Bliss on the afternoon panel of manufacturers who would tell Congress about the technology that did exist to let people with disabilities compete with the non-disabled. Barry described his electronic communications devices which enabled a non-verbal person to build his own vocabulary, compose conversations and play them with synthetic speech. Jim talked about the technology that electronically read a printed page to a visually impaired person, again using synthetic speech technology. I told how power wheelchairs, telephones, tape recorders and other electrical devices could be controlled by sipping and puffing on a tube if the person driving the chair had no use of their hands.

Perhaps our information was too technical for the congressman conducting the hearing. His first question was whether or not technology could be used to make people walk and talk. One of his aides whispered in his ear. He changed his line of questioning to whether people could use technology to be able to hold jobs. We assured him that this was more or less the idea that kept manufacturers like ourselves going — and borrowing from the bank to finance the products we made. In addition, we pointed out, some people with disabilities — like me — were very well employed. We even owned homes and payed taxes.

We ran out of answers when he asked why more people with disabilities didn't have the technology that would let them work. We tried the approach that the federal services did not allow a sliding scale of support so that a person with a disability could earn a living, but still receive assistance to cover some of the high costs of disability — like power wheelchairs, personal attendants and personal transportation. We even threw out some remarks about how it didn't make sense to spend $50,000 a year to keep a person on welfare just to save $3,000 or $4,000 a year by not subsidizing technology. His aide whispered in his ear. The congressman noted that we had digressed from the written testimony submitted prior to the hearing. Session adjourned.

Congress included some legislation to assist people with disabilities in each session through the next decade. On July 26, 1990, President Bush signed the Americans with Disabilities Act into law. ADA pretty much said that all the laws about accessibility of buildings and public transportation and equal employment opportunities and civil rights for people with disabilities that had been passed in previous years were really good stuff. We ought to enforce them. Actually, government entities — like the Department of Justice, the Architectural and Transportation Barriers Compliance Board, the Department of Transportation and a couple other agencies — re-wrote most of the previous legislation and published nice, thick books.

A number of us people with disabilities benefitted from the ADA. We were able to charge companies and legal firms pretty good prices to speak at their seminars or act as consultants. This somewhat offset our being snarled at by building owners and business people who thought it was going to cost a fortune to comply with ADA.

A friend of mine, speaking at a seminar sponsored by a large legal firm in Chicago, contended that the ADA was a full employment program for lawyers. He may have been right. A close family friend, who owns an over-the-road bus company, verbally attacked my father — who was obviously guilty by association with his disabled daughter. A team of lawyers had sought the bus owner out and told him it would bankrupt his company to make all of his buses accessible. Now, if he'd hire them.... Fortunately, this fellow wasn't as dumb as the lawyers thought he might be. He found that he could meet the requirements by modifying one of his vans for less than the lawyers would have charged for a day's work.

chapter 24

How the lawyers helped people with disabilities

L awyer-bashing is one of America's favorite indoor sports. It ranks up there with professional football and does have some similarities. The spectators pay to watch a bunch of people beat each other up using whatever tactics they can get away with while the players earn as much money in a year as the average spectator earns in a lifetime. The difference between the law and pro football is that football has referees and officials to keep some modicum of civility in the game. Also, you can go to a Chicago Bears game for about $100. You can't go to a lawyer for that amount — and the visit to the lawyer doesn't include hot dogs and beer.

In my 40 years of observing progress by people with disabilities, it's been obvious that the legal system in America has made various contributions. Law is a lucrative profession for those people who use wheelchairs and have the talent to become attorneys. Also, some disabled people have benefitted financially from the work of lawyers when they were awarded large settlements for the accident, malpractice or other cause of their disability. Of course, some of the lawyers that pursued these settlements are multi-millionaires from the 30% they kept from each settlement. Some of the disabled people got just enough money from lawsuits to cancel their social security support and were left with nothing — except having to re-apply for social security or state welfare — after the money ran out in a couple of years.

A person with a disability is a real boon for a lawyer. How can any jury be so coldhearted as to not award a large settlement for this poor victim, whose entire life has been ruined, who will never be able to do anything again. In court, as in physics, for every action, there is a reaction. My entrepreneurial friend, Dick DeVoe has picked up some pocket change over the years appearing as an expert witness in personal injury cases.

The juries were faced with a choice between old DeVoe — who'd built a profitable company and helped hundreds of other people with disabilities while doing it — sitting there in his wheelchair and the victim, sitting there in his or her wheelchair. DeVoe won the jury over more times than not. Besides, DeVoe is a very down-to-earth person. He always believed that there was a line between a fair settlement and rape of the defendant.

Dick DeVoe and I were bit players in one legal circus in the 1970's that cost taxpayers and people with disabilities millions of dollars. It centered around a charge of monopoly against Everest & Jennings. The event went on for a number of years and employed a lot of lawyers including some that worked for the United States Department of Justice.

E & J certainly did everything possible to avoid being a monopoly. Their products sure didn't show any noticeable application of state-of-the-art technology. Their customers pretty much hated them. On the other hand, there was no real competitor who supplied a wheelchair that the active wheelchair user could tolerate — and the funding agencies found it easier to approve the purchase of E & J wheelchairs. After all, that was what was prescribed by therapists, rehab counselors and dealers and people had been using them for years, hadn't they? Besides, a wheelchair is a wheelchair is a wheelchair.

Many of us who used wheelchairs were too occupied with things — like getting employers to hire us and finding the service entrance to buildings so we could ride on the service elevators with the garbage — to realize that our chairs didn't work too well. If you used a wheelchair for an active life, you more or less accepted that the upholstery would last six to eight months before it tore out. If you were prudent, you carried a spare axle or two in the tip-lever of your chair so you could sit on the ground and replace the axle that broke when you jumped down a curb.

When the big wheels started wobbling from side to side more than rolling forward, you sat on the floor, loosened the axle nut and tightened the axle bolt until it wouldn't turn — then backed it off a quarter turn. If you didn't do this every so often, the side to side action broke the balls in the wheel bearings. These bearings didn't have a long life expectancy anyway since they weren't sealed and tended to pick up enough dirt to lock the balls of the bearings in the race. At least you didn't have to worry about the persistent failure of the wheel locks when that happened because the wheels wouldn't turn. Also, when the wheels didn't turn, you didn't cut your hands on the chrome that was peeling off the handrims.

Not every wheelchair user was too preoccupied with other things to accept the fact that wheelchairs just didn't work very well. One leader of the movement to improve the quality and lower the prices of wheelchairs was Ralf Hotchkiss. Ralf had gone on to become an engineer after being paralyzed from the waist down in an accident. He also, it was reported, had served as an intern for Ralph Nader. Not only did he have the engineering knowledge to support his belief that wheelchairs could be stronger, lighter and cheaper, he obviously believed in consumers having a right — and an obligation — to challenge the manufacturing establishment. His close connections with the disability rights groups at the university in Berkeley, California enabled him to influence some others who used wheelchairs.

The Berkeley group was already tearing up some commonly-held theories about how people with disabilities should be cared for by society. In the first place, they seemed to be perpetually infuriated by the attitude that people with disabilities needed taking care of and said a lot of rather accurate things about the paternalistic, condescending attitudes of medical professionals, the federal disability programs, institutions of higher learning and anyone else who patted them on the head and said, "there, there."

They were doing such things as insisting that people with disabilities capable of living independently in a house in the suburbs, should not be confined to nursing homes. These Berkeley folks contended — and proved — that people with disabilities could run housing facilities, hire any attendant help needed and manage the whole living situation far better than the administrators of extended care facilities. They also felt that anybody with the intelligence to pass college courses should be allowed to go to the campus and do so — even if they did use a respirator to breathe or have an attendant.

The folks at Berkeley may not have invented independent living — part of that honor goes to some disgruntled students on the University of Illinois, who, in the 1960's, rented a house and hired graduate students to help them. Some part of that honor also goes to the work Lex Freiden spearheaded in Texas. The folks at Berkeley also weren't the first to insist on equal opportunities in higher education, which, of course had been done as far back as 1948 by some people at the University of Illinois. The one thing the folks at Berkeley did better than the others was raise enough hell to be noticed by the mass media.

When Ralf Hotchkiss paid less for an Everest & Jennings chair in England, Washington columnist Jack Anderson spent an entire column discussing how people in wheelchairs were being ripped off by this giant corporation. Actually, E & J — in the overall scheme of corporate America — was a pipsqueak. The chair that Hotchkiss bought was manufactured in Britain where labor costs — and pay scales — were lower. The whole and absolute fidelity of the reporting was irrelevant. Anderson's column resulted in that great American custom — righteous indignation.

E & J wasn't guilty of all the charges flung at them. It wasn't their fault that other companies that manufactured wheelchairs simply copied E & J's work and did nothing to make their product any more desirable than E & J's. E & J had not, however, done anything that would endear them to the users, dealers or purchasers of their products. Attempts to improve the quality of their products frequently resulted in problems for the users and dealers. Attempts to improve the delivery of their products made matters worse. Between installing a computer-operated manufacturing management system and building a new plant 60 miles north of Los Angeles, E & J managed to increase the waiting time for a wheelchair to be delivered from 30-60 days to 6 to 9 months.

The Jennings brothers were kind, compassionate men who reached into their own pockets to help individuals with disabilities. But, many of the middle-level executives kept dealers in states of rage. Dealers — who were being sued for taking nine months to deliver a custom wheelchair, thus making a child miss the first couple of months of school — really took offense at being told by one sales executive that, "you don't have any place else to go for products. You'll take what we can get to you when we can get it there."

One of the favorite activities of the MED group was to gather up quantities of rope, tar and feathers and other accessories needed for lynching and head for Los Angeles to declare war on E & J. Ken Sandler claimed that one of his customers waited so long for his chair that he started out being funded by Services for Crippled Children and was eligible for medicare by the time the chair arrived. Sandler also claimed that he was put on hold by E & J's customer service department for so long that the person who had answered his call had retired by the time someone else took the call off hold.

When the suit charging monopoly was brought by the Department of Justice, MED, like most dealers, faced a dilemma. E & J was a daily pain in the ass for each dealer. They were also our largest supplier. The only time we got any benefit from the company was when Sandler ordered Page 2 of the menu at one of the most expensive restaurants in San Francisco — and make that a Page 2 for each of 25 people. The only source of wheelchairs that could begin to meet our customers' needs was E & J. To replace the volume of their production, at whatever quality level, was physically and economically impossible for any manufacturer or group of manufacturers.

So Dick DeVoe and I ended up being the wheelchair users on one side of the lawsuit, with dozens of wheelchair users on the other side. We knew we didn't have a choice other than to defend E & J — unless we wanted our customers to be forced to use wheelchairs designed to transport patients in hospitals. Strong orderlies couldn't push those chairs, let alone anyone with a disability being able to make them move.

Most events in a person's life can be a learning experience if the person allows it. The monopoly suit was very instructive. It gave us the opportunity to observe the legal system in action. The Justice Department had a large team of lawyers assigned to the case. E & J responded by retaining a large Chicago legal firm.

The J Department lawyers literally hid behind potted palms in hotel lobbies to pick up information from conversations among manufacturers and dealers. The whole industry was accused of collusion when we accidently held a meeting to talk about the need for international standards for wheelchair manufacturing. We all just happened to be at the same conference and we all had felt for a long time that some standards should be developed. It was kind of like a movie when lawyers from E & J's firm rushed into the room, grabbed the meeting attendees and wisked them off to different parts of the hotel just before the J Department boys came up the hall.

The Chicago firm boys had their own methods of practicing the law. Some of these included spreading a rumor that one of the J Department boys had been found in a very compromising position, clad in very little other than his membership in the bar association — in an extremely public place.

The case was a short course in depositions. Those of us involved learned that a deposition is a legal way to spend a lot of money on lawyers who ask questions of witnesses — who are told by their lawyers to stick to the old Geneva Convention routine of name, rank and serial number. Requests for information beyond that brings on instant amnesia in the witness. Depositions were made more fun by the Chicago legal experts. They knew that holding the deposition in an unheated room in February in Chicago was a good start to dampening the enthusiasm of the J Department man. Then they gave the J Department guy a metal folding chair with legs of uneven lengths and fired up the most foul-smelling cigars to be found. The J Department man decided to conclude the deposition when the Chicago lawyers held a conversation about whether or not that was the J man's car the police were towing away from the parking lot.

The suit by the J Department inspired every dealer dropped by E & J — for matters considered by the dealer to be insignificant, like not ever paying for products, tripling the suggested list price and fabricating the information on their dealer application — to bring civil suits. Participants in this legal feeding frenzy were sentenced to five to seven years of giving depositions and appearing in courtrooms.

Dick DeVoe and I rather enjoyed our all-expenses-paid vacation in Sacramento so we could testify at a civil trial. Dick was pretty disappointed that he never got to testify. As the second witness, I was coached by the Chicago firm to dress like a sweet little lady in a wheelchair who only left the house twice a year when the ladies from the church took her to the park. The prosecuting attorney started to lose it when he asked if E & J had given my wheelchair to me without charge. I told him that my wheelchair was manufactured by E & J's quickly emerging rival, Invacare. He asked if I knew of any other companies that manufactured wheelchairs. When I reached the 17th name on the list of 38 companies I'd memorized, he lost it. He yelled. I cried. The judge threw the whole mess out of court.

Eventually, E & J won all the civil cases. The J Department decided they couldn't prove monopoly, so they slapped an injunction of E & J. Under the terms of the injunction, E & J had to set up a subsidiary company to market E & J products manufactured in Canada and Europe — which turned out to be not to the liking of the U. S. users, but that was just as well because the tariffs imposed on those products made them too expensive to compete with the products manufactured in the U.S. E & J also had to refrain, for ten years, from buying any companies in the business of manufacturing medical equipment. No one in the industry could remember E & J ever buying any such companies before the injunction either.

While the United States Department of Justice was fighting to protect the citizens with disabilities by breaking up E & J's non-monopoly, the private sector was doing what comes naturally — responding to increased market demands and customer insistence for better products.

E & J's market share of commodity wheelchairs — those used for short-term rental, transport in hospital, airports and amusement parks and depot chairs for the VA — was seriously diminished by the emergence of a major competitor. Invacare Corporation just sort of sat in Elyria, Ohio and manufactured sturdy, cheap, clumsy wheelchairs until an aggressive — OK, arrogant — ex-Marine Captain named Mal Mixon checked his personal agenda. Mal, who claimed to be part Cherokee Indian, had made it from an Indian reservation in Oklahoma to Harvard. After serving in combat in Vietnam, he returned to Harvard for his MBA and set forth his personal agenda.

By 1978, Mal was 38 — and his agenda was that he would be president of a company by age 40. People who know Mal or have worked for him can list a lot of the man's traits. Patience is never mentioned. He took a loan out against personal assets, used his superb sales skills to talk some Cleveland businessmen into backing a loan and bought Invacare in late 1979 — just under the deadline for his agenda.

Mal approached the wheelchair business with the same style he'd used in Vietnam with the marines. He was going to wipe E & J off the map. There is no record that he ever used napalm or fired an assault weapon at the E & J plant from a helicopter, but he did charge up a lot of figurative hills, firing figurative ammunition, taking no prisoners and leaving few survivors. Invacare soon owned the commodity chair market. Onward and upward to prescription wheelchairs, Mixon bellowed. That took a few years longer. Attack the power chair market, Mixon commanded. That took even longer.

While Invacare engineers were dropping from Mixon's forced march into the prescription wheelchair market, some people out in California were starting the real revolution in manual wheelchairs. Jeff Minibraker and his buddies thought they knew what they wanted in a manual wheelchair. After all, most of the people in the company named Quadra used wheelchairs. Therapists, who knew the appropriate therapeutic design for wheelchairs, tended to either pass out or leave the room when presented with a Quadra wheelchair. The thing was ugly. It was made of aluminum instead of nice, shiny-chromed steel — and the damned things didn't even fold! And the Quadra was so lightweight that it would probably slip out of reach when people transferred from the toilet to the wheelchair — or they might go zinging off the sidewalk into traffic because the things moved too easily.

When the Quadra was presented to dealers, most of them suppressed equal parts of laughter and groans. Nobody would buy a chair that didn't fold. They couldn't fold it to put it in their car. Besides, everyone who knew anything about wheelchairs knew that the X-brace on the chair allowed it to flex on uneven surfaces. Furthermore, these dealers had warehouses full of parts for the E & J chairs and were being forced to stock Invacare to answer customer demands. Quadra was another in a long line of strange attempts to change wheelchair design.

The only people who didn't think the Quadra chair was ugly and unfunctional were very active people with disabilities. They saved up their own money to buy a Quadra when therapists wouldn't prescribe them to assure payment by third party payors. So many active people switched to the Quadra that the chair was stuck with the description, "sports wheelchair" — which, of course, guaranteed that funding agencies wouldn't buy them. Can't spend scarce health care dollars on frivolity like sports, can you?

Not long after Quadra and several imitators started showing up at trade exhibitions, a gal named Marilyn Hamilton expressed her feelings about what a wheelchair should do. Marilyn had taken a fall while hang gliding and ended up paralyzed. She and two of her friends scraped together what personal funds they could find, located a small building and designed a new wheelchair. Like the Quadra, it was made from lightweight metals used in the aircraft industry. This chair didn't come with shiny chrome plated frames either. And it didn't have a dignified name — like Premier or Elite. The inventors chose to call it the "Quickie." They've always claimed the name resulted from the quick response of the chair to turns and propelling motions, but they also didn't mind the immediate applications of the obvious double entrendre.

To shorten this part of the history of what people with disabilities did for themselves and others, all that is important is that both E & J and Invacare refused to buy Quickie Designs when the company's sales rapidly outstripped its ability to keep up. In a few years, Quickie had taken over so much of the prescription chair market that both E & J and Invacare copied — or tried their best to copy — the Quickie design. The copies never really threatened the Quickie market, a fact that drove wheelchair marketing people, including me, to drink a lot.

In the end, Dick Chandler bought Quickie and added it to his Sunrise Medical family of companies. Chandler set the durable medical equipment market in an uproar by his success — which seemed to be rooted in his strong belief that the customer was the best source of input to any given product. He accidently set a another precedent for the industry by hiring the best people he could find for each position — without any concern about the fact that a lot of his employees had disabilities. Chandler just assumed that these folks knew how to out-design, out-sell and out-market the competition and that they'd take care of how they did it without any worries about job accommodations.

Ralf Hotchkiss was probably the key to starting the whole uproar in making wheelchairs usable. Dick DeVoe and I, who had imagined this guy to be a cross between King Kong and Lucifer, found out that Ralf is a soft-spoken, gentle, caring man. He has spent many years traveling to third world nations, teaching the natives of those countries to make wheelchairs from materials easily found in their area. He's developed ways to fabricate chairs that don't require complex machinery and processes, such as tool and die work — often not available in those areas. As a matter of fact, he's now one of Dick's and my heroes.

chapter 25

Taking technology to the people

The legislation and the multiple bureaus in Washington committed to helping the disabled through technology were having the usual effect that legislation and federal bureaus have on the lives of the people they were established to serve — full employment of bureaucrats. No significant rise could be discerned in either awareness of how technology could overcome disabilities nor in access to those technologies.

Still, many dedicated people were doing some innovative things in using state-of-the-art technology to let people with disabilities succeed in education, jobs and everyday life. But the people who were making things happen still didn't have an effective way to compare notes. There was a lot of reinventing the wheel — or, in most cases, the whole wheelchair.

Many people believed the field of rehabilitation engineering had potential to change life for the disabled and that the opportunities for reaching the people in the street would be greatly increased by moving out from under the shelter of federal agencies. In 1979, five men set the stage for a grass-roots, independent organization that would become the training grounds for not only rehab engineers, but therapists, doctors, manufacturers and others, whose professional lives revolved around transfer of technology to overcome disability. The men were Colin McLaurin, Jim Reswick, Doug Hobson, Tony Staros and Joe Traub.

Each man had a long history of achievement. Colin McLaurin, who headed the University of Virginia Rehabilitation Engineering Center, was considered one of the founding fathers of rehabilitation engineering. "Mac" believed that the logical discipline of engineering should be applied to solving matters such as how to make wheelchairs last longer and respond to the user's needs. Jim Reswick, who probably exceeded the level of genius in electronics, had been a pioneer in functional electronic stimulation of paralyzed muscles and introduced engineering to rehabilitation. At this time, Jim was head of the rehab engineering department at Rancho Los Amigos in Downey, California. Jim was as into theory as Mac was into mathematics and physics. For example, Jim used his theoretical abilities to build an efficient, full-sized car which operated totally on battery-supplied electricity. Jim discovered that he had left out one small detail — how to turn off the ignition — which he solved by driving around the parking lot until the batteries were drained.

Doug Hobson, of course, had dedicated his life to applying engineering principles to seating and positioning and dynamics of the human body to optimize function and lessen the chances of physical problems such as skeletal deformities and pressure sores. Tony Staros and Joe Traub had been part of the group for years. Tony, as the VA official who dealt most closely with rehab engineering and Joe, as the rehab engineering liaison for civilian government bureaus, such as NIDRR.

At an interagency conference on rehab engineering in Atlanta in late 1979, the five put together a last-minute meeting to talk about forming an organization that would be a clearinghouse for information, a vehicle for training and a stimulus to cross-disciplinary interaction.

The initiation of RESNA, the Rehabilitation Engineering Society of North America, wasn't anywhere near structured and orchestrated. Mac, Doug, Tony and Joe sort of worked behind the scenes, letting Jim explain the concept to a couple of hundred people who'd been drawn to the meeting by conversations held in the hallways. To tie in manufacturing and disabled technology users, they let me have the mike for a while, knowing that letting me near an audience was good for 45 minutes of explanation on any topic.

Jim and I were convincing evidently. At the end of the meeting, most of the people in the room signed forms that said they wanted to be members of RESNA. Funding for launching the society was taken care of by Bob Graebe, who had developed the strange-looking, but effective ROHO pressure-sore prevention system for wheelchairs. Bob walked up to the stage and handed me a personal check for $1,000.

Ray Cheever, who had started *ACCENT on Living* magazine using only the funds he and his wife, Grace, could raise through advertising, loved the idea of RESNA. When Ray likes something, he throws the full support of his magazine behind it. After all *ACCENT* had long been telling the story of how people with disabilities succeeded. A few articles in *ACCENT* put a certain amount of concrete in the concept of the RESNA idea. After all, once something appears in a national magazine, there is an incentive to make it really happen.

Like MED, RESNA was more smoke and mirrors than reality. For the first five years, the organization had no staff, no office and almost no funding. All it did have going for it was success. Bits and pieces of RESNA were located wherever they landed. I had one file drawer for RESNA at the MED office and many piles for RESNA in my house. Jim had more files and piles at Rancho.

Our long-suffering MED attorney, Bill Delp, pointed out that we should take care of legal matters — like by-laws, incorporation filings, etc. Since he brought the topic up, he got to do them — pro bono. When Jim left Rancho to bring the VA up to speed on technology in Washington, we found we'd shot ourselves in the foot. Among our rules were that an employee of a federal agency couldn't be an officer of RESNA. No problem. Colin McLaurin stepped in as president. Now RESNA was spread out between California, Illinois and Virginia.

Mac was more organized than Jim and me, so RESNA began to gain more structure. We even had a conference the year RESNA was officially founded — 1980. It wasn't really a RESNA conference. It was the Canadians' turn to host the international conference on rehabilitation engineering and Mickey Milner, another leader in the field from the University of Toronto, incorporated RESNA into the event.

Mickey Milner was no less a character than Jim or Mac.

Born in South Africa, Mickey had emigrated to Canada. There, the good Dr. Milner had attacked the problem of giving kids with disabilities the chance to grow up to be ordinary people. His fertile mind spewed forth ideas on how to get kids mobile, let them communicate and compete in school — and usually he got the Canadian government to pay for it. Being in a room with Mickey was very much like being with Dorothy when the tornado picked her up from Kansas and deposited her in Oz. Mickey could always "tweek" any circumstance until it became "tickety-boo" and he could never be accused of fitting his own description of the epitome of reticence — being too shy to "say boo to a goose." He attacked RESNA with his customary energy and, by 1981, the society was independent and lived up to its claim of serving North America. After all, the name of the society did include North America — and Canada is a significant part of that continent. In addition, the Canadians were frequently ahead of the U.S. in rehab engineering — in fact, the U.S. had stolen Mac and Doug from Canada. At the end of the conference, RESNA had 300 members.

Mac passed the title of President of RESNA on to Don McNeal for the next year — which was probably a good thing for Mac's financial picture. When he was awarded the first E & J Lectureship in rehab engineering, he handed the $1,000 check to me to deposit in the RESNA account. Whenever the RESNA bank account was a little low, Mac made a deposit to keep us going.

Don's international reputation in several areas of rehab engineering, most particularly functional electronic stimulation, has always been overshadowed by Don's California beachboy good-looks and overwhelming charm. Those of us involved in RESNA have always claimed that the number of female members of RESNA quadrupled when McNeal took over as president.

Dudley Childress must have been in one of his states of his mind being elsewhere when a topic was discussed when he agreed to chair the first RESNA meeting. I wasn't paying attention when I agreed to help him. The logistics were challenging. The conference was held in Washington and Dudley and I were both in Chicago. RESNA had a small grant from a federal agency to help with the conference, but the agency had mandated that the money be used to pay a consulting company that the agency had long supported — sort of "keep the money in the family."

We've always pointed out to Dudley that he had hair on his head when the conference began, but the experience rendered him nearly bald. That may have been an exaggeration, but the experience did render him speechless for most of the week the conference was held. The two of us huddled in out-of-the-way corners of the hotel a couple of times a day to compare the income from registrations, meeting and exhibitors' fees with the expenses charged by the hotel. Don McNeal has never let me forget that he was faced with a very surly board of directors after I cancelled lunch for their meeting. The day's financial balance didn't cover a couple dozen sandwiches.

Don retaliated by threatening unspecified physical harm upon my being if I did not remain as secretary-treasurer for another year. The man is brilliant. He realized no one could ever follow the accounting method I used for that conference. Dudley's and my tendency toward frugality paid off. At the end of the conference, RESNA had $40,000 in the treasury to tackle the next year.

Don, being well grounded in business as well as research, grabbed me a few months later and we went off to Washington to hire a professional society executive to run RESNA. Pat Horner, whom we hired, improved accounting and record-keeping immeasurably over my methods. Pat could find any balance or fact immediately in her books. I could rarely find the books.

The concept of RESNA was working well. At conferences, people from Atlanta found that people in Seattle were working on the same challenges and that the work of both groups progressed much faster when they compared ideas. Therapists learned that engineers had a valuable contribution to make to a team working with a disabled person to figure out how to make a work station usable, for example. Engineers found that dealers weren't crass and commercial, but were really pretty helpful gals and guys. Manufacturers got new ideas from the engineers — and engineers learned the real, gritty story behind how a product makes it to market. Getting the people who used technology to overcome their disabilities involved had a few rough spots in the process.

It wasn't that there were no people with disabilities involved in RESNA. Margaret Pfrommer, Larry Scadden, Peter Axelson and I were there from the start. Although they valued our opinions, the other RESNA members thought of Margaret as a source of design input, Larry as an engineer with vast knowledge in technology for people with sight impairment and Peter as a talented mechanical engineer with a tendency to design unexpected products. Who, for example, but Peter would believe that hundreds of people, paralyzed in most of their bodies, would want a mono-ski that you could sit on, strap yourself in and zoom down a snow covered mountain at 60 miles per hour? Peter was right. Other skiers with disabilities took to his products with such enthusiasm that they often beat Peter out of the gold medals at international competitions.

In the first years of RESNA, members who had disabilities joined because they worked in some area of rehabilitation engineering. About once a year, one or another disabled consumer activist group would exhibit the same blind spot for the physical status of rehab engineering professionals who used wheelchairs and charge that RESNA didn't involve any people with disabilities. Those of us who rode wheelchairs or followed a white cane down the street would shrug and get IBM to give us money to sponsor selected people with disabilities to the next conference. Some such consumers found the field interesting and went into some aspect of it as their career. Others preferred to gripe that no one cared what they wanted in technology. This attitude was nicely dubbed, "the I Want a Sip and Puff Pony" syndrome by Mac — which was his way of pointing out that not everyone's desires for technology to overcome their disability is realistic.

The tensions between some disabled consumer advocacy groups and RESNA were always just under the surface. Chairpersons of the Consumer Involvement Committee, originated by Ray Cheever, publisher of *ACCENT on Living*, usually burned out after a term or two until a blond dynamo from Minnesota, Rachel Wobschall, grabbed hold of the committee. Rachel quickly pulled together all of the previous work on consumer involvement, used her experience gained in establishing one of the most successful state technology education programs and turned the committee into a powerful voice to support technology. The fact that Rachel has cerebral palsy makes it hard for other consumers to claim no one listens to a person with a disability.

chapter 26

The marketing exec on wheels

While RESNA was taking technology to the people in the street — who happen to have disabilities — I was having adventures in the commercial version of taking technology to the people.

New climates and circumstances in the rehabilitation equipment arena had forced MED to alter its course. Changes in reimbursement for products and services, increased competition and other factors began driving small, independent companies into ever-deepening financial woes in the early 80's. One by one, MED company owners realized that the proverbial window of opportunity was open for them. If they were to secure their family-owned and operated companies in a manner that would guarantee security for the family, the time to sell to a larger company was now.

Our arch-rival, Abbey Medical, having been taken public by the charismatic Dick Chandler, was no longer pictured by MED members as "Shabby Abbey." Even Dick DeVoe refrained from his only known effort to bring religion to the group with his invocation, "Hail Mary, full of Grace. Please make Abbey second place."

In a few years, Abbey owned eight of the MED companies. MED retaliated by bringing aboard new MED companies in the same cities. For about five years, MED sales people, who controlled which company was used by critical accounts, had a hey-day. Many of these sales people became owners of new companies that competed with Abbey. DeVoe's crew found financial backing and opened a store a couple of blocks closer to Craig Rehab Hospital than the store Abbey bought from Dick. Though rather hard on the nerves of those playing this game, the winners were people with disabilities. There's nothing like good, clean, cut-throat competition to improve service and lower prices.

This was not a secure situation for any of us. While some of us were sneaking around behind potted palms in hotel lobbies negotiating with National Medical Enterprises to buy the whole MED group — whatever it was composed of that day — another MED faction was doing the same number with another potential buyer. Our poor MED member in Cleveland and Akron accidentally sold out to NME even as the other deal was going through.

The corporate chaos temporarily strained friendships as well as nerves. It totally shot our long-term planning out of the water. When the dust settled, MED was sold to a pair of adventuresome businessmen — whose names I've forgotten — who were really buying up a number of companies so they could, in turn, sell them to Beverly Health Care for a quick profit. In addition to being jealous because I didn't think of the scheme, it became obvious to me that I was no longer running MED. We'll never know whether the new group wanted an M.B.A. with balls, rather than an M.S. with boobs, whether the group wanted to take a new direction or whether my tendency to say what I think, damn the torpedoes and full speed ahead put me in the out-group. Whatever the reason, MED and I decided to part company.

After playing around with some possible jobs in Chicago, it seemed like it would be fun to take Mal Mixon up on his offer to move to Cleveland and help him build a rehab products division. Considering that Mal and I share equally large egos, quick tempers and world-champion degrees of stubbornness, the move could have been ill-fated from the start. Instead, it was a chance at an advanced degree in an entire new area involved in progress for people with disabilities.

Mal was still running the company the way he'd run a marine platoon — or whatever they called what he'd done in Vietnam. He'd line up the troops, tell us which hill we were going to capture that week— usually the hill was code-named Everest and Jennings or Sunrise Medical, but he was impartial and got around to every company in the industry — give us an impossibly short length of time to destroy the enemy, then leave it up to the troops to do it. It turned out that this decision was a wise one on Mal's part. He never did get the hang of things like scheduling design and production. He certainly never bought the idea that you should finish a product before you began to sell it.

Everyone who uses a wheelchair or other orthotic device — any device which substitutes for a body function, like mobility or speech, as opposed to a prosthesis, which replaces a body part, like an artificial leg — should work for a company that manufacturers those devices. I'd used a wheelchair since I was 13 years old. I'd sold them, researched them, argued about their design and cursed them. Going into Invacare as a marketing executive made me realize rather quickly that I didn't know anything about wheelchairs.

Being a marketing exec at Invacare seemed to cover a lot of ground. The job description was basically, "do it now." My friend, Mary Ann, who has spent her entire career as a marketing executive for one of the most venerable of all advertising and marketing companies, Leo Burnett, often points out that what Invacare called marketing bears little resemblance to the definition used by the rest of the world. For one thing, there was no dividing line between "marketing management" and "product management." This gave you the chance to utilize many talents including some that you had to fake.

A typical day of a marketing person (MP) at Invacare might start out with glancing through a three-inch-high stack of engineering change orders. These dealt with earth-shattering matters — can we substitute the purple lock nuts that the suppliers accidently sent in for the yellow ones? — and had to be initialed by marketing, engineering and quality control. Halfway through the stack, the phone would probably ring and quality control would demand that you come down immediately to the assembly line in the plant. Arriving at the assembly line, one might find that manufacturing had again made a change which resulted in the seat height of a power chair being 22" from the floor. You'd stop the line. That always proved you were serious about the problem getting changed. Besides, it was the only power trip you'd have that day.

While the line people wandered off to the cafeteria for

coffee and cigarettes, MP would attack manufacturing to try to get across the idea that an inch and a half of additional seat height would make a big difference to the person using the chair. They might not be able to get off the toilet or out of bed into a chair that high. Then MP would rush off to a meeting with engineering, production, purchasing, quality control, distribution and sales to hear why the product MP was pushing for introduction couldn't be ready in time. Seems there was no time in tooling to make the necessary fixtures to bend the frames....

Back in MP's office, three calls from frantic salesmen needed to be returned. One salesman couldn't sell the new wheelchair model because the customer only wanted blue frames. How come we can't have blue? Our competitor does. (Because a special color adds a hundred dollars to production costs, you idiot. Go sell red. We have red.) The second salesman would have promised that we could make a power chair that had a top speed of one-and-a-half miles per hour — and if he didn't get it by Tuesday, he'd lose the sale. The third salesman found that all of the tires on the power chairs in his southwestern territories were exploding in the heat.

Throwing notes to follow up on whether engineering could change the electronics on the power chairs to restrict the speed and check with purchasing on the power chair tires and wheels, good old MP would rush off to another meeting about how many of which products we were going to sell in which months of the year. Manufacturing did have to schedule and tell purchasing what supplies to buy a couple of months ahead of production.

After learning that the printer messed up the new

brochures that had to be shipped by this afternoon, glancing at sales figures — and making a mental note to duck because Product A was way below forecast — MP would scribble some notes comparing why our product was far superior to the competition. Scribbling the notes had to be interrupted by running down to quality control to see exactly how many trips around the bumpy track of the testing carousel, while loaded with a 200 pound dummy, our competitor's chair had survived. I don't recall that anyone ever transferred this information to the user, but it did show us the weak spots in chairs so that engineering could work on making them last longer in real life.

About this time, when MP was wondering if lunch would be part of the day's schedule, somebody would probably rush in asking if — just this once — MP could take a group of dealers on a plant tour. Hopefully, MP would remember to pick up the airline tickets and agenda from MP's secretary before she left for the day. Marketing was scheduled to spend about a quarter of their time in the field. You had to know what was going on out there, didn't you? Besides, salesmen and women got brownie points from their accounts when folks from the corporate office showed up and schmoozed the hospital staff.

It was a fun job. I liked it. I'm not sure anyone could do it for a lifetime and survive, but it gave me a chance to see what obstacles exist between the customer's dream of having a good, durable wheelchair — that does everything including some things that are impossible under the laws of physics — and the manufacturer's delivery of the product. It also was a lesson about an invisible barrier that keeps people with disabilities from being served as well as they could be by technology.

First, there's the matter of profit. Without the motivation of profit to drive companies to beat — or at least survive against competitive companies — no progress would be made toward improved products. The not-for-profit, publically-funded efforts to get technology to the people who ride down the streets in wheelchairs has never produced a usable product.

Profit has a double-edged effect. In the federal-funded controlled market of assistive technology, companies must keep tight control on costs by limiting changes to products and purchasing materials. Unlike the auto industry, where consumers make the choice of what they'll pay for a car, the wheelchair industry must stay within the guide lines of what the Health Care Finance Administration (HCFA) will allow.

The auto industry is a good analogy for another barrier that prevents people with disabilities from access to the latest technology. Nearly all people working in the auto industry drive cars. When I was at Invacare, I was the only employee at the corporate offices that used a wheelchair. Good old Jim Knaub, our west coast Rehab Area Manager used a chair — very well, in fact, as he supplemented his income from sales for Invacare with winning most of the marathons in the country and appearing on TV and movies.

Most of the people who manufactured wheelchairs in the Elyria plant not only had never used a wheelchair, they'd rarely seen a person in a wheelchair other than Jim and me and Jim's contribution to product design was all based on what the wheelchair athlete needed. Actually, his more memorable contribution was a universal swooning of every woman in the customer service and parts department when he visited Ohio. He dispelled any questions that sex appeal can't make a wheelchair go totally unnoticed.

Even Jim's charisma didn't win all Invacare employees over. Well, the head of the parts department had good reason to not adore Jim. Every time he visited, he left with half the parts department having been bestowed upon him by the female employees.

Basically, though, there was an under-current that the customers were a pain in the ass. Even I thought some of the customers were a pain in the ass. Pat Nally, the fiery vice president of sales, once verbally shredded me — this was an equal opportunity company where women had an equal chance to be shredded — when he found out how I'd solved problems with one customer. When I got sick of this guy whining in my phone, having to send him parts for his power chair because he kept hearing a funny noise and, finally, sending an engineer to California to listen for the funny noise, I called my salesman in the area.

"Go over to ABC Medical. Buy an E & J power chair. Take it to the VA and get that SOB out of our chair and give him the E & J. Put it on my marketing account."

As it turned out, E & J was more angry with me than Pat. They retaliated by turning one of their nightmare customers over to Invacare. Some of these nightmare customers were a result of lack of education of the customer on how to use a chair. I must admit that it never occurred to me that anyone would take a shower in a power chair until one of our best dealers and I became detectives to find out why the operation of the chair was very erratic. Even though our electronics were protected against moisture, we hadn't planned on them being exposed to a 20-minute bath every morning.

Some of the customers were pains because they expected more than mechanical devices can deliver. One of our east coast salesmen deserved a medal for bravery when we sent him in to convince a woman who weight 210 pounds and was 4' 10" that the reason her chair pushed hard was because the flesh of her hips was poking out through the spokes of the large rear wheels. Teenagers were hard to convince that slamming the joystick on a power chair into reverse to stop at the bottom of a steep hill has the same effect as throwing your car into reverse while driving at 60 mph.

Drunken driving was as prevalent in wheelchairs as in cars. Invacare drop-tested the chairs to determine what areas needed strengthening, but the lab drop tests never totally simulated a 200-pound man driving his power chair full speed off a 10" curb and landing in the street — repeatedly. Urine collecting in the power chair control boxes was easier to solve. We moved the control boxes to the back of the chair. After all, anyone can have an accident.

Too often, however, "the customer is a pain in the ass" attitude could carry over to customers who had legitimate problems. A family, whose neighbors had raised $8,000 for a power wheelchair for their child, should expect that the chair would operate more than four hours a day. The back uprights and footrests assemblies of manual chairs should stand-up under normal use. And the tires on your power chair shouldn't explode even though it was attributable to the wheel manufacturer changing the material composition to something that got soft in any temperature over 70 degrees. Of course, all manufacturing defects were corrected by the company and many employees went beyond their normal jobs to help customers. But the frustration factor built up on the part of both the customers and the manufacturer's employees.

"Quickie" was one of the most foul obscenities that one could utter in our plant. Marketing attributed the success of that chair to something called "customer mystique." That's probably an accurate assessment. Quickie manufacturing was controlled by people who not only used chairs, but were well-known athletes and leaders in the disability movement. Customer feedback from active wheelchair users was the basis of their business, rather than something added to an already established design and manufacturing program.

There were more subtle, less concrete indications that lack-of-understanding of the needs of people with disabilities can exist if manufacturers and customers aren't sharing experiences and thoughts. It seemed pretty thoughtless, for example, when someone covered the ramp leading into the main plant with a lovely, deep-piled carpeting. The result could have been used for a Paralympic event — struggling through carpeting while negotiating an eight-degree grade.

It also dumb-founded Mal every time I became either hysterical or abusive when mandatory management meetings were held in a country club that had 17 steps to the entrance and no bathroom on the first floor. He found it unbelievable that I would object to being carried up uneven stone steps by a few strong men, attend a four-hour meeting and drive 18 miles home to go to the bathroom. The country club, he pointed out, was in financial difficulty and we owed it our support as good community citizens. To his credit, the problem was eventually solved by a driveway that went up the hill and only one step had to be negotiated.

The old adage that familiarity breeds contempt is wrong

in some cases. In the case of Invacare salesmen, familiarity resulting from traveling with me bred a lot of understanding that they used in their jobs. It also bred a conviction in their minds that I could go anywhere and do anything they could — or they'd tear the place down.

Big Freddy Jensen at least convinced one hotel that he was tearing it down one piece at a time as he strode up and down hallways, slamming doors in a search for a room with a bathroom door wide enough for a wheelchairs. Turns out the hotel's definition of "wheelchair accessible" meant the room was next to the elevator.

On another trip, my six "Rehab Area Managers" would only accept an offer to spend a relaxing afternoon on a yacht in the Seattle River if I agreed to go along. Getting up a six-foot ladder to climb over the side of a boat is not wheelchair accessibility at its best. The guys solved that. They found a bosun's chair, picked me up and plopped me in it and hauled me aboard. They did dangle me out over the water until I agreed to stop yelling at them for losing products from their sample accounts, but it seemed like a fair trade — especially since I panic at heights. It's always nice for a girl to be accepted as part of the gang — although I could have done without the frequent, crowd disrupting game of six tall, attractive males charging across hotel lobbies shouting, "Come on, Jan, let's go chase girls!"

People working together — disabled and non-disabled — can solve a lot of problems. The Invacare sales force drove minivans. A minivan seat is too high to transfer to from a wheelchair. The big, athletic salesmen solved the problem by picking me up and setting me in the van. One less athletic type drove around until he found a very high curb which put the seat at transfer level. The funniest solution, though, was worked out by our man in Detroit. He found two planks, used them as a ramp to get my wheelchair in the van, then turned his head as I wriggled between the driver's and passenger's seats to land in a safe passenger position.

We weren't perfect at Invacare, but we honestly tried to improve products, especially wheelchairs. We forced a very competitive situation in the power chair market which resulted in at least four major companies battling one another to gain the greatest share of the market. This battle resulted in vastly improved electronics incorporating microprocessors. Within a few years, power wheelchairs included features that had been discussed and dreamed of for several decades by those in federally-sponsored research.

Microprocessing not only meant that the driver of the chair could adjust speed, turning speed, acceleration, deceleration and other options to suit his or her needs, but that people with severe manifestations of cerebral palsy or traumatic brain injury could, for the first time, use a power chair. The electronics could be programmed to sort intended motions from tremors and unintended motions to the joystick. Time delays between activation of the joystick and movement of the chair allowed for restricted response time common in traumatic brain injury. Children could safely use these chairs to let them learn how to be independent — and experience what the distance across a room actually felt like.

Best of all, perhaps, the competition among major companies and the rapid advances in electronic technology brought the prices of power chairs down. Slowly, the intent expressed in the halls of congress in the 1970's — to use technology to help the handicapped — was becoming a reality.

chapter 27

Where we are now

Over forty years have brought a lot of progress in allowing people with disabilities to live normal lives. The term normal is subject to suspicion, of course. For one person, getting into a wheelchair in the morning, going to the same job for 30 years — if that condition ever returns to our nation — being able to make the payments on the mortgage and save enough to send the kids to college is normal. For the next guy, leaving his wheelchair at the bottom of the mountain and climbing to the top is normal. The freedom to choose one's own definition of "normal life" is the ultimate goal. It's all a matter of perspective.

Perspective is needed in all areas of life with a disability. Following the onset of a disability, a person has to decide whether his or her goal is total physical restoration of the body to the shape it was in before the disability or whether to accept the fact that things have to be done in different ways while pursuing other goals. Neither choice is wrong. What is wrong is the acceptance that health care professionals, teachers or family should make the choice for the person with the disability.

A vast industry has grown up around disability. Researchers, intrigued with the potential of computers to process huge amounts of information, are trying to develop programs that will allow a clinician to measure how much movement you have in each muscle of your body, throw in your family history, what your neighborhood looks like, what kind of books and TV programs you watch and, for all I know, whether you've ever had incestuous thoughts about Uncle Herman. Then they'll be able to push a button and the computer will print out exactly what you'll be able to do and how you will live.

While this could save you a lot of time thinking you'd like to be an overseas television correspondent, when the computer has just proved you will have to be content with a job in telemarketing, it may not be the best start toward satisfaction. At least, the researchers point out to me, we've come a long way since the days when the doctors and therapists looked at you and — while thinking to themselves, "boy what a mess this guy is" — said, "we're not sure what you'll be able to do. Probably not much." Now they have a whole computer full of information on which to base their prognosis of "not much."

We claim progress in that we've moved from not providing any education for children with disabilities to a system that qualifies an amazingly high number of children for special education. Back in the one-room country school I attended, Mrs. Pope treated Attention Deficit Syndrome in her own way. She explained that the kid would sit down and read a book — or else. We were always afraid to explore what "or else" might be.

Now we support a system called special education. Basically, special education separates out all children who are different from their peers and puts them in curricula that prove to them that they are different from their peers. Since these kids are "physically challenged," let's don't mess up their little minds by intellectually challenging them. Every so often, a kid escapes the special ed system and goes to regular school. There, he finds that the other kids pick on him because he uses a wheelchair or talks funny. Then he notices that kids pick on other kids because of where they live — or the clothes they wear — or whatever occurs to the little devils. The disabled kid is likely to figure out that life is cruel, but that's not particularly because of his disability.

ADA mandates that people with disabilities should be provided access into all stores and restaurants. But it can't deal with the fact that people with disabilities often complain that waiters and clerks in stores speak to the nearest by-stander to find out what the person with a disability wants.

This attitude shouldn't come as a surprise to anyone who's been through a rehab program — or most areas of our health care system, for that matter. Legislation can't prevent many members of the public from viewing people with disabilities as patients, with all the burdens that title carries. A lot of work is needed to overcome the idea that disability belongs in the medical model.

If you're a patient, the medical world has a set procedure for helping you. To determine how you want to live, the medical staff is going to "staff" you. This is an activity conducted in a room in which you are either not present — or if you are, you have the same amount of input as the wall chart showing the major muscle groups of the body. The physical therapists talks about your biceps and quadriceps, the occupational therapist talks about your ability to dress yourself. The nurses talk about how often, how much and how easily you urinate and whether you have red spots on your butt. The doctors mutter about prognosis, the recreational therapist says you have a lousy attitude toward team sports and the social worker says you're hostile. The final arbitrator in this group, the case manager, says she doesn't care how or what kind of wheelchair is best for you, you're only authorized for such and such an amount of money.

Now, don't you feel just like a competent person and more in charge of your own destiny?

To try to change the image of people with disabilities, many go out and join a disability activist group. There are very good ones — although you really should choose your friends more on the basis that, like you, they're Chicago Bears fans, hate Chinese foods and think having a good time isn't complete without a hangover the next morning. Or, maybe you're more into politics, computer hacking — you get the idea.

Some disability advocacy groups actually reinforce the isolation of people with disabilities by hating all persons and things not disabled or designed for the disabled. It's hard to enjoy what you can do when you're spending all your time griping about what you can't do — like going to a specific restaurant when there are dozens of others you could go to.

It's hard to sort out feelings and harder to be an independent thinking individual. But, then, considering the general population, why should folks who have a disability be different. As a nation, our attention has focused so much on recognizing minorities, that probably the majority of the population now belongs to a minority. We live in a morass of subcultures.

Recent studies say African-American children are punished by their peers for doing well in school because doing well in school is a "white man's" thing. Some factions of what people with disabilities choose to call the "disability community" criticize athletes and others with disabilities, who blend into business and professions, as unfairly projecting the image that having a disability isn't such a big deal. The crips who "pass" for regular folk criticize the physically challenged who insist in reveling in tales of how hard life is.

It's making this person with a disability — who usually calls herself a crip, if pressed to provide a label — confused. Am I supposed to assume that anything that goes wrong in my life can be blamed on discrimination toward the disabled? Did Invacare lay me off because they disliked people with disabilities? Should I have sued Mal for loudly announcing on many occasions that I was his "token crip"?

Invacare laid off more than 25 executives — proving that they are a company ahead of their time by downsizing a couple of years before Ameritech, IBM, Amoco and the rest of corporate America did the same thing. Was Invacare guilty of politics by choosing the people to be the downsized? You bet they were. As for Mal, I shouldn't have sued him — just punched in the portion of his anatomy I could most easily reach. Was he discriminating? No. He insulted men, women and dogs with an impeccable degree of equality — a trait for which he should be forgiven in light of the fact that he brought competition to the wheelchair industry, which, in turn, made better, cheaper chairs available to more people.

Even I am unable to realistically determine whether I've ever been discriminated against in employment because of my disability. Like most crips, I think I have, but, on the other hand, the arguments from both me and my employers would be too emotionally based to be fairly judged.

Am I Pollyanna — the little girl who found something good about even the most hideous things, like calves foot jelly? Yes. I'm Pollyanna because there have been a lot more good things in the past 40 years of progress for people with disabilities than bad. We can make a list of them. We can even compare advancements for people with disabilities with advancements for other minorities — like African Americans and women.

Let's start with education. People with Disabilities (PWDs) can now enter any college or university they choose. Hopefully, their success won't be hampered by their earlier special education. Like African-Americans, kids with disabilities have won the right to be put on buses for a couple of hours and go to the "school that's best for them." The results in this category come out a tie — kids with disabilities are assured an education by law, but that education could be made more effective by treating each child's needs on an individual basis.

PWDs have won recognition for their ability in sports. The Paralympics are moving closer each year to being totally incorporated into the Olympic Games. Sharon Rahn Hedrick won the first gold medal awarded by the International Olympic Committee for a sport in which a wheelchair is used — in Sharon's case, to burn up the track in racing. Sharon outclassed the runners who use only their feet in the Olympics held in Los Angeles in 1988. Nice analogy with other minorities here — how do you think those people using wheelchairs in commercials and TV dramas got there? Just like Michael Jordan, many PWDs began as sports stars.

In the area of access to public facilities, the PWDs haven't advanced as far as the African-Americans. A lot of times, PWDs still can't get on the bus — let alone ride on the back of it. And Jesse Jackson would have every news service in the country covering an episode in which an African-American had to ride on the freight elevator after coming in through the back door.

Employment opportunities are a draw for the two minorities. Employers bemoan the fact that, in order to hire a minority person, you have to find one with the skills to be an engineer or one with management experience or whatever. People with low-level skills and low-level education land in low-level — or no — employment. This is a matter that has to be fixed by better education and training.

Technology is a factor that makes or breaks employment and life opportunities for members of any minority including PWDs. If you learn computer skills, for example, your proficiency in the area will negate many of the drawbacks resulting from the disability. The increase in jobs in the service industry means that people with developmental disabilities — or whatever current politically correct term encompassed slow learners — have more opportunities for employment. The service industry jobs don't pay much, but that's a concern of a lot of former corporate executives at this time, too.

Progress has been made in applying technology to overcoming limitations resulting from disabilities. A lot of this progress has been a by-product of the explosion of developments in electronics. Microprocessors can make your power chair go straight down an angled sidewalk, climb steep slopes and even tell you why your wheelchair is acting sick. The same technology in augmentative speech can let you speak Japanese even if you don't understand what you're saying. Products are on the market to let you live alone, including a robot that asks you if you took your medication on time and lifts that let you put yourself in and out of bed.

Will government programs pay for these micro-chip based equalizers? Of course not. But, again, there is an optimistic future. Most of these things are so handy that they're sliding into the general market — which means they'll keep getting less expensive and more available. In five or six years, the only product area to be termed "assistive technology" will probably be wheelchairs.

There has been some progress in developing programs that allow people with disabilities to take jobs and work their way off support programs. Too few people know how to use the Social Security Administration's complex methods of doing this and too many disabled people find that they still are imprisoned by a lack of available health care insurance because of their disability. The lack of available health insurance is exacerbated by the fact that legislators chose to leave health insurance companies exempt from any part of the ADA.

But the bottom line is that over the past 40 years, thousands of people with disabilities have, in succeeding in many fields, made it possible for other PWDs to have more chances to do more. Why were some successful and others not? Why did Ray Kroc make the whole world want a Big Mac while Sam Mutts couldn't keep his sandwich shop open for more than four years?

Should we suspect that success or failure has something to do with the complexity of factors that makes each individual unique? Could it be that we are more in control of our own lives than we realize? I hope the government never issues a grant to study and evaluate those factors and put them in a computer program that will analyze what makes a success or failure. In the first place, the study would never reach the people on the street. It would have to be studied by other researchers, who'd probably discover flaws in the original research which would indicate that, if we really wanted to be a success, we should sit under a special light for three hours a day and avoid eating anything but organically grown vegetables. Then another government study would prove that the lights caused skin cancer and the organically grown vegetables resulted in birth defects.

Maybe it would be better if people with disabilities could be declassified as a group, the health care profession encouraged to stop treating disability and just treat people. We could let people with disabilities handle their own lives by dividing the money spent by the Health Care Finance Administration on supervising the lives of PWDs, which would give every one of the PWDs covered an annual income of about $45,000 a year. And — for all the do-gooders and social saviors who dedicate their lives to helping the unfortunate cripples — we could take the federal funds to study how PWDs live, how they should live and how more studies can help them live that way, give it to the do-gooders and send them off to places like Bosnia, Iran and Columbia — led by Jerry Lewis.